WHITE MISCHIEF

THE TRUE STORY OF THE WOMAN WHO MARRIED A KENYAN TRIBESMAN

CHERYL MASON

SUMMERSDALE

Summersdale Publishers
46 West Street
Chichester
West Sussex
PO19 1RP
UK

Printed and bound in Great Britain
by Selwood Printing Ltd., Burgess Hill

ISBN 1 873475 29 2

Cover design by Sophie Sitwell

Dedication

To the memory of Elsie Partridge; Nan.
May you rest in peace.
April eighteenth, 1911 - August third, 1995.

White Rose

They placed a crown of thorns
Upon our saviours head,
Then pushed them down so deeply
That his heart, tears of blood it shed.
Only the blind people could not see them,
And laughed at him instead.
They nailed him tight to a cross,
And waited for his death,
Then took him to a tomb to lie and be forgotten.
But in seventy-two hours from the crown of thorns
Had risen the purest of white rose
The world had ever been given.

Cheryl Mason, 1992

This book is also for my three fine children; Stevie, Tommie and Chloie Mason. They continue to surprise me with their strength of character. Their lives have been a rollercoaster of emotions and changes, throughout which they have remained ever constant in their loyalty to me. I love you with all of my heart.

For Mike Mason, who has been a good and trustworthy father for both of my boys and Chloie. I thank him for all he has done and still regard him as a wonderful friend.

Thank you Andy, Pat, Helen and Simon Lockhart, Ruth Rowland and May Stayton; all of whom are fine friends of my family. Thank you all so much for your lasting support.

To my sister Richelle Nash-Edwards, her lovely children; Julia, Jemma, Kimberley, Kristal, Charlotte and Elliot. I pray they all find happiness. God bless.

Thank you Lance Stewart. Be happy.

For my husband, Daniel Dikola Lekimenju. Forever I will love you from the bottom of my heart. You gave me back that fighting spirit within. I thought I'd be lost forever, now I would be lost without you.

You have taught me the true meaning of the word love. There are no way in words to tell you what you mean to me. I thank God for you.

To all the Samburu Masai People: Kore Anakitabu nkichono naajonge takaai. From Nicmarie.

Acknowledgments

Amy Mandeville
My editor: Whose sheer hard work has gone into the production of this book. I wish all authors could have an editor equally good. My heart felt thanks go to her.

Stewart Ferris
Who I have always felt believed in me and this book. Thank you for giving me this chance. And for that typewriter.

Alastair Williams
For being calm when I have been temperamental during the times I lost faith in myself. Cheers.

In truth I am indebted to all three of you. Thank you all so very much.

Contents

Chapter One	9
Chapter Two	17
Chapter Three	26
Chapter Four	37
Chapter Five	44
Chapter Six	52
Chapter Seven	60
Chapter Eight	70
Chapter Nine	81
Chapter Ten	93
Chapter Eleven	103
Chapter Twelve	112
Chapter Thirteen	120
Chapter Fourteen	127
Chapter Fifteen	137
Chapter Sixteen	143
Chapter Seventeen	151
Chapter Eighteen	159
Chapter Nineteen	174
Chapter Twenty	182
Editor's Note	189

Chapter One

Maybe if the sky hadn't been so blue on that morning, or the grass so green. Maybe if my new kitchen was a disaster. If my husband was cruel or if my children were monsters. Maybe if any of these things had been true, that morning wouldn't have become the vortex destined to suck in my life and spit it out on the hot sands thousands of miles from anything I had ever known.

My contemporaries can always seem to remember where they were when they heard about the Falklands. People of my parents' generation remember when they heard of the first bomb leaping out of the dark skies over London. For me the watershed was a single summer morning.

It wasn't mere unhappiness. Unhappiness seems to have carved itself out a niche as a rather proactive emotion, for me anyway. I had been trained from an early age that it was to be endured, and that true character came from sitting down when every fibre of your being is begging you to run. Childhood had become an exercise in immobility. Unhappiness would not have provided me with enough fuel for my get-away.

No, I believe that my fire came from a feeling so foreign that the only logical response was flight. The motivation was pure selfishness and its price has been staggering, as have been the rewards.

So much of my life, from the very beginning, was taken up by taking care of other people. Staying with my mother as a shield from my father when I could have gone into care. Staying with my infant brother to protect him from my mother when my grandmother would have taken me in. Marrying a man I didn't love to spare my children the difficulty of not having a father. That morning the time came to care for myself.

'Shit!' I screamed, as the hot coffee spilled over my hand and onto the white oak of the kitchen table. Annoyed, I slammed down the cup, spilling more.

'Cheryl, please. Look at the mess. Must you? And do you really need more than one mug a day for your coffee? Look at all these.' He attacked two offending coffee cups in the sink. 'Why don't you wash up one instead of grabbing another?'

'Well, Mike, God in all of his goodness blessed me with more than one.'

'More than one what?'

'Cups, Mike, cups. If I only had one cup, I would wash it and use it again straight away. But I don't have one cup, I have twenty. When I've finished with cup number twenty I can go back and wash them all. But maybe you're right. Maybe we should give all of our glassware to charity and have one cup between the five of us. Then the cup would always be washed up. When we have guests we could all use straws the kids steal from McDonald's. What do you say Mike?'

'Oh you. Sarcasm is the lowest form of wit.' I mouthed this silently while he said it, my back to him.

He left the kitchen and blew his nose for the hundredth time that day in the old grandad handkerchief that he kept stuffed down his baggy old transparent boxer shorts. He had grown very overweight since we moved to the Isle of Wight. His hairy pot belly oozed over his shorts. When he bent over I could see his cleavage.

I looked around for a dish cloth to clean up the neglected coffee spill. Mike dashed past me busily, balancing the laundry basket against his belly as he let himself into the yard to collect the washing. I watched him as he came back in the door, beginning to fold the clothing before he had put down the basket and snapping at Tommie and Chloie over his shoulder,

'Tommie, don't do that. Chloie, stop that now, what have I just told you?'

No wonder men have affairs if this is what it is like to live with a housewife, I thought.

'Would you like a cup of tea, Mike?'

'Oh, alright then. You're not going to use ten cups are you?'

'Would you like a divorce Mike?' 'Yes, alright then, I'll have a mug of coffee, but try not to spill it all over the place this time.'

'Mike, I'm speaking to you.'

'Yes, I'm listening,' he says, walking into the morning to discipline the children.

It is the 1960's, not that anybody in my family has noticed. We live in a flat with two dark rooms, an outside loo and a scullery yard. Our only running water is from an old yellow Butler sink with a cold tap. For the cleaning of clothes we have a stone boiler. My sister and I sleep together in an iron framed single bed with an ill-fitting mattress. It is covered with a red bedspread, supplemented with moist overcoats in cold weather. It never seems to be warm. There is a taxi rank at the end of our road. Many a sleepless night is spent counting the reflections of their lights on the ceiling, rolling by endlessly.

The summer before I left for Kenya, something in me snapped. It had been difficult having Mike around the house all of the time. He seemed to see me as an object to sit by prettily whilst he pottered around the house like an old woman. I kept on telling myself that I should be grateful for how he made my life so easy by taking care of all of the details of a family and house, expecting me only to be there.

He had briefly held a position with the Royal Mail when Chloie was nursing and even then he would pop in around eleven o'clock to feed me a big fry-up and straighten anything that needed fixing. At first it was sweet and I was grateful. Eventually he became a cloying presence that I couldn't shake. A ghost that was always hovering at my shoulder.

I can't say that there was anything particularly different about that morning. I got up as usual, took Stevie and Tommie to school. Mike and Chloie went to a playgroup where Mike volunteered a few times a week. I found myself alone again in a spotless house. I went for a walk, browsing through the shops for nothing in particular. I passed through to the beach and watched the ocean, smelling the briny water and admiring the murky green colour that comes with the clouds.

Without warning a sense of helplessness came over me that was so severe I started crying, bringing my hair forward around my face to hide the tears from the tourists. All of the frustration with the absolute tediousness of my life rushed to the surface and became a burden too heavy to be borne. I wanted more than anything to be free, to leave behind the emotional wasteland of my marriage.

Slowly I stopped my tears, soaking them up with the sleeve of my jumper. Rooting in my purse, I found a piece of scrap paper to blow my nose in. I wiped under my eyes to clean up my mascara and patted my hair into place.

I got to my feet and walked back through the town to the bank, withdrawing five hundred pounds. Next I stopped at the travel agents, where I bought a one way ticket to Jersey. I wouldn't have to go home for my passport. I stopped at Woolworth for toiletries, cosmetics and a small bag. I went to the local charity shop to get some clothes to pack in my new bag.

I called Mike from the pier before the ferry was due to leave. 'Hello Mike. If you want the car it's at the Ryde pier. The house, the car, the children, they're all yours. I have taken five hundred pounds and am leaving for Jersey. I may not be back.'

I hung up on his laughter.

I arrived in the afternoon, stepping off the ferry with dozens of families with small children. I didn't stop once to think of my own small family. The day was wet and windy but I felt warm and happy, free.

I walked until I found myself on the steps of the Porthole Cottage Hotel, run by a diminutive Irish woman named Maureen. She asked me my business, which I quickly told her, relieved to have a friend, needing an ally. She offered me a position by her side running the hotel for the summer. I turned her down, wanting to remain at loose ends, for now at least.

After a few days an emotional plea came from Mike over the radio. I ignored it. I had begun to see another man named Joe. He was a bit younger than me, with money which he seemed to enjoy spending on me and good food. I didn't fancy him particularly, but he was different and this made him attractive.

After a while I found myself beginning to feel things again. I would see a child's blonde hair and catch my breath thinking, if only for a moment, that it might be Chloie. I would see a pair of boys walking together, one smaller than the other and have to stop myself from running after them to see if they were mine. I made the concession to my family of calling Toni, a family friend.

She said I didn't sound at all myself and she hadn't realised I was so down about my marriage. She assured me that if I would only come home she would take me somewhere with her. After coaxing me for a bit she began to threaten that she would come and find me if I did not come home on my own.

I was missing my children and really didn't want to create such a big fuss, and promised to return to the Isle of Wight, which I did shortly after. I knew only too well the independence that I was throwing away, but the price of this seemed too high.

I arrived home to very grateful children. I doubt that I will ever be able to fully explain to them why I abandoned them or even why I returned. I may never know how much all of the events of the last few years have affected their tender minds. I can only hope that their scars do not go too deep.

Mike seemed largely indifferent to my return. He boiled me up a cup of tea and asked few questions. It was if I had been out doing the weekly shopping. He stopped only to say that he was sure that the rest had done me good and I would now start feeling better and everything would be O.K..

I told Toni of Mike's apparent lack of emotion and she had me pack my bags for Portugal.

Chapter Two

Looking back, I think that Toni's primary motivation in the trip was to suss me out to see if I would be a good companion for her to take to Kenya. I tried to tell her that Mike and I had gone on our honeymoon in Northern Africa and had a miserable time and I simply had no will whatsoever to visit that Continent again. Still she would insist.

I remember the conversations. She would go on and on about 'her boys', a group of Samburu Masai dancers in Kenya. She bought gifts for them while in Portugal and insisted that I would love them and would love Kenya if I ever went. If I admired a beach, Toni would say that the ones in Kenya were better. If I liked a certain food, the food in Kenya was tastier. She kept on about one 'boy' in particular, a Dikola, saying that if she could marry him she would. There was no distracting her from her own personal promised land.

During the trip to Portugal I had begun to understand certain things about Toni and her relations towards men. Because she was my friend and had paid for the trip, I didn't feel that I had any right to say anything to her about the way that she conducted her private life. In fact, I largely left her to her own devices until she began to insist that we go back to the flat with the men. I informed her in no uncertain terms that this was not acceptable and I would have no part of it. Surprised at my insistence, she conceded and followed me back to our hotel, apologising. I put it down to stress about the death of her husband and the alienation of her children and forgave her.

I am sitting under the big table. Large, dark beams of wood cross under it, forming an X. I have been sitting in this inaccessible oasis for hours, the crossbars forming deep welts in the backs of my legs. I have adopted an old chair back as a child, and she shares my space with me. I find an old rag and wrap it around her like swaddling clothes. My baby is of lovely dark wood. I will always protect her. She will never lack for anything. I will rock her and rock her. The monsters daren't come near my baby and I, shielded from the world, we survivors.

A conversation invades the world of my new family. My happier, whole family. I try not to listen, but it stays.

'Are you still under there?' Nan asks. I don't answer. It's not the world I want.

'Jean, this child has been here all day.' Rock, rock.

'Don't fuss,' answers a second voice, 'she's alright, good as gold and quiet as a mouse, she is. Hardly know I've got her.'

'You must feed her, Jean.'

'No, what for? She never makes a fuss, so I don't bother. Besides, Richelle took all I had.'

A shouting match ensues, and I turn my attention to the child in my arms who has begun to cry. I kiss the burled wood, rocking, rocking, cooing away her tears.

In my crooning I beg the world, I beg myself, I beg the scrap in my hands to please make the noises go away.

My relationship with Mike rose from the ashes of the marriage to my first husband, Robert. Robert was an odd, vindictive man, set on repeating a family history of early fatherhood and abandonment. He gave me two lovely sons and then left me, with very little remorse and almost no future contact.

I was naive going into the relationship. I had only had one serious relationship, with my boyfriend Lance, before settling down with Robert at the age of twenty-two, and that partnership had been equally strange.

Lance was my first love. I had a school-girl crush on him beginning in my early teens. He outclassed me by far, having a father in the Scotland Yard and a stable family. My family was considered, and probably was, quite lower class and not at all suited to the neighbourhood the council had placed us in.

By the time I was sixteen I was taking a majority of the responsibility for my younger half brother, as my mother had become an alcoholic and my sister had left to move in with my natural father and then my maternal grandmother. I was also responsible for a great deal of the household chores, as well as my schooling, which had recently finished, and a part time job at the hairdressers and then at the fish shop. I was fed up.

I met Lance after I had left home in a fit, throwing most of dinner all over my stepfather. I was sitting outside the steps of the local church, crying. I saw Lance walking towards me down the street. I tried to hide behind my hands, but he came and talked to me, comforting. He explained that he would have liked to have spoken to me before, but was intimidated by all the boys who made a habit of following my chest home.

We became close very quickly, going everywhere together. We avoided sex for a long time because I was frightened of it and I had my mother telling me that I would be sure to go mad if ever I slept with a man because I was so funny about being touched.

Finally we did become intimate. I was completely frigid and it ended in tears. Lance stuck by me, however, determined that he could cure me of my fear and neurosis.

Eventually life with my mother and her second husband became too much for me and I left, hiding in Lance's bedroom for a time before I could convince him to come with me to get a bedsit in London.

During the time that we stayed together I was becoming increasingly more violent, until finally he left. We gave it a few more tries over the years, feeding off each other's neediness. He saved me from a suicide once and then tried to enter into a suicide pact on another occasion after some nude photographs of me were plastered over various men's magazines. Finally we parted, quite bruised for all of the miles. When I met up with my first husband, I was feeling quite ready for something that was, on the surface, less damaging than the tug of war I had been involved in with Lance.

I met Robert on Hayling Island when I was working a summer job on the Isle of Wight. My sister was working on Hayling and invited me to stay one weekend when the staff were having a big fancy dress party. Robert was at this party.

I left the next morning for my own job, and left there a few days later, being concerned about the flat I had in London. Robert tracked me down through my sister and we fell into a relationship. We were together for all of the wrong reasons, and the partnership fell apart after five years.

Because I was used to being on my own, having left my mother to her second abusive husband when I was sixteen and living with my own flighty husband, I was not as stricken as I might have been when Robert did leave permanently. My eldest son felt his absence, however.

I was beginning to come into my own. I had a house in Bromley provided by the council and was following my love of the stage in classes offered by the local college. Both of the boys were in day school and I was adjusting well to my status as a single mother of two small boys. I understood my children's need to have a father and, in deference to these needs, I still dated, hoping for a man who would be a good father and provider, who would make every effort in the world to be kind to me. I soon met Mike.

He worked at the chemists down the street from me. He was a pharmacist's assistant and normally stayed at the back of the shop. It was the flu season and I was coming in quite a bit to pick up the various formulae required by children at this time of the year. Mike heard my voice one day and liked it so much that he came to the front of the shop to see who it belonged to. He fancied me and admired how well behaved my children were. He proceeded to come to the front of the shop from then on whenever he heard my voice. I never really even noticed until he began to ask me out.

I didn't fancy him. He was heavy through the gut, and wore his hair in a sloppy outdated style. His clothes were that of an old man and, because of the extra weight, he was jowly. I let him down gently and repeatedly.

One evening he stopped by my house, having found the address from my pharmaceutical records. He said that he knew I hadn't been well and he was stopping in to check on me. I invited him in for a coffee and a chat for his trouble. We talked for three hours.

He told me that he was the product of a couple with very Victorian values. His parents had been loving towards each other, though not necessarily towards Mike. His father was in the RAF, then became a maintenance engineer and his mother had been a nurse and secretary. He had nursed them both until their deaths from cancer, his mother dying eighteen months after his father. He had been married for five years to a teacher, but they had unsatisfactory sexual relations largely based on his low sex drive. I admired his frankness and thought that he was perfectly harmless. In fact, I thought that he might have been a homosexual or simply asexual.

At the end of the evening, in front of the boys, he suggested that we all go to the zoo together. I couldn't disappoint my children and, against my better judgement, I said yes.

He began to spend a lot of time with the children, taking them various places and being sweet to all of us generally. I helped him with his appearance, making him look closer to his age of thirty two years.

The boys called him Dad, and eventually getting married seemed not so much a choice as an inevitability.

Chloie was born a few years later, and after that we moved, against Mike's better judgement, to the Isle of Wight, where he has remained largely unemployed.

I wish that things could have been different with us. Even today I consider Mike to be a valuable friend. I can't say that he is a bad person. I can't even say that he was a bad husband. Neither of those things is true. My problems with Mike stemmed more from the fact that we had differing expectations about what we wanted from a marriage and from life.

When I first met Mike he was everything that I needed. He had a decent job and a small inheritance. He loved my children and treated them as though they were his own. He was never cruel or even inconsiderate. He was lonely and getting to the point that he knew that he wanted children and a family and would need to start soon. I was able to provide him with both of these things.

In retrospect, none of these reasons is good enough to base a marriage on in this day and age, when people need a different glue to keep them together other than a sense of social or family duty. Most couples today marry for love and if they leave each other, do so after they have already started to separate from each other mentally, to drift apart. We never drifted apart. We had never really been together in the first place.

Chapter Three

After returning from Portugal, life became very routine. Mike and I lived our separate lives. I took a job at the local theatre as social secretary and often came home late. I would lock up the theatre and then drive off to find a lonely beach somewhere. I would cry and consider the possibility of leaving Mike. Then I would remember my children and realise the impossibility of such an escape.

I would cry to God to forgive me for being so ungrateful and for not being happy with Mike. Forgive me for getting exactly what I asked for and wanting to throw it away. I asked God to teach me how to truly love properly, as my parents had taught me only sex and hate. I prayed for a person I could love mentally and physically. I asked for all of these things and more. I cried them all into the winds at the top of my voice as loud as I could.

On one of these nights I arrived home at one thirty in the morning, letting myself in via the front door without a sound. I checked the table for a note from Mike. At this point most of our communication was occurring through little pieces of paper placed conspicuously, as we studiously avoided any significant contact. The note on this occasion advised me to call our family friend Toni as soon as I got in, regardless of the time, as she would be waiting up for me. Curious, I rang her.

'Well,' she said, 'I have chatted with Mike tonight, and he says he's happy about the tickets to Kenya I have booked us as your Christmas present. I am telling you early because you need to get your vaccinations before you travel. Mike says he is happy about you going and has no problem with looking after the children for three weeks. I've booked us in for January 2nd. We're off, kid.' She then had a fit of girlish giggles, having said the entire spiel all in one breath. I said nothing.

'So, how do you feel about coming along?'

'You're joking.' It was the only thing I could think of to say.

She assured me that she wasn't and gave me the list of vaccinations I would have to get in preparation for the trip. Her enthusiasm is contagious and I found myself thanking her and telling her how appreciative I was. She promised to call again in a few days.

Still, there was the niggling resentment with both Toni and Mike that they had taken it upon themselves to direct my life in this fashion. I wondered if they had thought of my children and how they might feel with their mother leaving them again. After I had come back from the trips to Jersey and Portugal the children had become clingy and were less willing to give me space, much less three weeks abroad.

It seemed so incredibly far.

I felt terribly guilty about leaving my children. I didn't like to leave them alone for any amount of time, particularly after the insanity of my escape to Jersey. In the end I decided that I would just have to do my best to make the three weeks separation as easy on them as possible.

Every day that I got another vaccination I would come back and report to the children about it. I would talk easily with them about my leaving and return. Chloie and I would sit and discuss aeroplanes and how they worked and how Mummy would be leaving in one but would return home soon. I made tapes for her of me telling funny little stories so she wouldn't feel quite so neglected.

Toni had Christmas with us that year and came bearing piles of gifts and enough food to feed a dozen of us. She cooked us a lovely dinner. It was a pleasant change and we were thankful for each other's company. She left on the 27th of December for

London and I followed on New Year's Day to make the connection to Kenya.

My family saw me off at the pier. Chloie was sitting on my hip and I cried into her chest that I did not want to go and would miss them all so much. The boys assured me that all would be well and they would look after Chloie. I still felt uneasy, as if things would never be the same after my return.

I boarded the ferry to Portsmouth and locked myself in the toilet to hide my tears. I told myself what an adventure it would be. I thought of how for three whole weeks I could be myself. I wouldn't have Mike or the children to worry about. I would spend my time in Kenya finding myself and deciding on the direction of the rest of my life. My tears receded as a knot of fear and excitement tied itself in my stomach.

I wet the bed again. Mummy is angry. Her mouth curls cruelly, eclipsing her face into a mask of cruelty, pain and ugliness. She is screaming, biting, hurting.

I sob as she kicks me around the room like a football instead of a child. Something dead and not a part of her. The world explodes as my face is pounded mercilessly into the wooden arm of a chair. I hear myself crying and feel the blood running down my face in great rivulets. I watch my Mother's face, and wince as it changes again. She is standing looking at me. Watching.

She walks away, returning with a wet bit of flannel which she presses over my mangled face. 'It's not so bad as a nose bleed,' she croons, as if I had just taken a nasty tumble down the stairs or been bullied. I close my eyes and seek refuge in the blackness. What else is there?

Toni and I were travelling with her brother, Brian. Brian was a very laid back man who was coming along as sort of a chaperone. He would also prove himself to be an excellent mediator between Toni and me.

Toni was terribly bossy at the airport, organising Brian and me. I told Brian that I had never seen this side of Toni and he laughed, saying that this was only the beginning and he was awfully glad that I was coming along to take some of it off of him.

Toni seemed quite flustered, blowing hot and cold and rushing around unnecessarily. She was short tempered, but I put it down to having such a long journey to endure.

The plane trip was pleasant and I just laid back listening to Toni nattering on about 'her boys.'

It helped to pass the eleven hour trip. I explained to her that I did not intend to get as involved with the Masai as she was. I wanted only to spend my time unwinding by the pool with a good book and some sun cream. Toni said that this was perfectly acceptable as long as I would at least say hello. I assured her that I would.

The plane touched ground in Mombasa at six in the morning. Even at this time of day the heat was intense and a shock after coming from the winter chill of England. Waiting to go through Kenyan passport control, I was very uneasy. A few very black faces stared at me continuously. I was unnerved by the idea that one might take a fancy to me. Toni was making some sort of a fuss with the trip representative and Brian was rolling a fresh fag. I was too tired to pay much attention to either.

We finally made it through and boarded the bus to our final destination. Toni fidgeted, saying that she had a feeling that this trip was a terrible mistake. She gave no explanation as to why she might think this. I didn't understand what she was rabbiting on about, and was too tired even to pretend to care.

The landscape outside the bus was odious. All dirt and dust and shacks made of any garbage that was easily transportable. A sign along the road read 'Born to Suffer'. Children chased alongside the bus, half dressed. Old weathered faces stared up at us resentfully. I was glad to be locked away from them. I half heard Toni moaning about some beads she had dropped onto the floor of the bus. Brian, rolling another fag, told her not to worry about it. I ignored her.

We pulled into the hotel, terribly posh and in stark contrast to the hovels we had just passed. Some small black men rushed out to the bus to get our luggage and the three of us went to the lobby to sit with a fruit drink and wait whilst they sorted out our room, which we would be sharing. The sultry heat did little to revive us, but I liked it and the luxurious lethargy it brought. Frogs croaked from a nearby pond and some yellow birds hovered in the trees in the garden. There was an organic clicking noise which I couldn't place that seemed to fit the mood. I watched the staff as they went about their duties. No one was rushing. Everything was very laid back and it calmed some of my nerves.

After a few minor misunderstandings we where shown to our room. The Porter seemed to think that Toni and Brian were my parents, much to the chagrin of both Toni and, to a lesser degree, Brian.

Toni changed and left for the beach with Brian, leaving me to shower and rest in bed with a book. Later in the evening I joined Brian down at the pool for a cup of tea. He told me jokes and made me laugh and relax a bit. Two hundred yards from where we sat was an outdoor arena where the locals would come to entertain the tourists with traditional African dances.

Some of the dancers passed by, largely ignored by Brian and I. We figured that we would be there for another three weeks and they would be bound to be there again.

Much to my embarrassment Toni called across to me at the top of her voice to come over to her. Everybody was looking at her and then me and I felt myself colour. Toni was wearing tight flowered leggings with a matching fitted top.

'Hurry Cheryl, they're thirsty,' she beckoned.

'Get over there quick, Cheryl, Mummy's calling,' laughed Brian, rolling another of his smelly cigarettes.

I silently cringed over to where Toni stood, holding court with the profusely sweating dancers.

When I joined her she gestured to the tray of about twenty drinks that I was to distribute amongst the men. I felt terribly clumsy and out of place amongst this forest of tall black men. Toni's demands were getting louder and surlier and the natives looked on in bewildered amusement. They were talking amongst themselves in their own language and giggling. I tried not to notice.

One of the young men approached me saying 'Come, come. Come and say "jambo" to all.' He led me along a dimly lit path to greet the others. I eventually found myself alone under one of the party lights that hung in the trees lining the path. I watched the patterns that the lights were casting on the dirt path, occasionally glancing up to watch Toni talking with some of the tribe. I must have been terribly tired, as I stayed this way, quietly secluded for a fairly long time.

Without a sound a shadow fell across the path before me. I looked up quickly, startled. I found myself gazing directly into the face of a very tall, slim Masai Samburu warrior. I caught my breath. He looked magnificent in his beads and bright red kanger, the wrap traditionally worn by the Masai. I could smell the red ochre from his long plaited hair. His body smelled faintly sweet, not sweaty. His red and orange face paint was done with such care, he was fascinating to look at and like nothing I had ever seen before. He was staring at me hungrily, his eyes so big I thought they would swallow me. He reached out as if to touch me and then broke into the most beautiful smile I had ever seen. Oh, I thought, you've finished examining my soul.

He took my hand and stepped forward, shaking it. He introduced himself as Dikola. Something stirred in me and I dropped my eyes to the ground, refusing to look at him. I tried to grab my hand away from his grip, but he simply held tighter, clasping my hand between the two of his. I could feel his eyes looking at me, gently mocking, daring me to look at him.

'You did not watch the dancing tonight,' he said, finally.

'No,' I agreed, 'I was not interested in watching your dancing, I'm so sorry. When will you dance again?'

'You can come tomorrow to the marina and watch our dancing there.'

I found myself responding that Toni was the boss and any decisions were up to her. I had very little say in anything we did. To my surprise he went straight up to Toni, asking her to please bring me to the marina the following day, as I had not seen the dancing that night.

'Yes, yes,' she said, paying little attention, more interested in her own agenda. 'Dikola, I have some gifts for you, including a radio. Do meet me outside the hotel at ten tomorrow morning.'

'Yes Toni,' he agreed, 'but please bring this girl with you again.' Toni disregarded what he said and turned to another of the young men, effectively closing any conversation.

Dikola returned to my side, shaking my hand for what must have been the third or fourth time. He promised he would come for me at ten o'clock the next morning and, flashing me his brilliant smile, he disappeared down the dark of the dusty path.

After he had gone I approached Toni asking why Dikola had been so determined that I see the dancing.

'He was not,' said Toni, 'Dikola is a good Christian boy and he would never say such a thing.'

'He just did,' I insisted.

'Don't be so silly, Cheryl,' laughed Toni, 'the tourists ask the locals for chaperones, not the other way around.'

'Silly woman,' I thought, 'I didn't imagine it,' and turned heel towards the hotel.

Chapter Four

I started to feel uneasy about the meeting with Dikola. It haunted me throughout the night. I fell asleep after ages of tossing and turning only to wake up in a cold sweat in the middle of the night, feeling that he was in the bed with me. My heart palpitated, and I could hear the blood rush in my ears. I started to hyperventilate and rushed to the bathroom, so as not to wake up Toni or Brian. I found a bag and breathed into it, calming myself. My face was bright red and I was covered with goose bumps. I climbed shakily back into bed, trying not to think of the look in Dikola's face and his big brown eyes. The hungry wolf, the starved rat, the killer insect. I didn't sleep anymore that night.

He arrived early at the outside bar the next morning, with two of his friends, Mike and Douglas. He was much more shy in the daylight than he had been the previous night, looking up only occasionally. He said hello and shook my hand. He was very polite with Toni. I pretended not to notice his shy, childlike glances.

Toni was showering them with the gifts she had purchased in England and Portugal. I could see that Dikola was trying to be interested, but his heart was not in it. Toni had given Mike and Douglas walkmans, but had given Dikola a radio. I asked him why this was and he explained that he did not like to keep music for himself but rather liked to share it with the other boys. They all seemed more interested in the gifts than in any real friendship with Toni. I thought this a shame.

Toni disappeared for a time, leaving the four of us to talk while Brian shuffled good naturedly towards the bar. They asked me many questions about England and my life there. I told them that I was thirty three and they all laughed and said that couldn't possibly be. I must be in my twenties. They said that they had just assumed that Toni was my mother, leading to another bout of merriment.

I picked up my camera to take a picture and they suddenly went deathly serious. I put the camera back down and told them that I did not want the bloody photograph and pulled a face like theirs, making them snigger again. 'Oh good,' I said, 'you won't break my camera lens now.' I think that our friendship was sealed from that moment on.

We finished our beers as Toni returned to leave with us for the dancing at the marina. Because she was so tardy we found that we had missed the festivities. Dikola suggested that we head down to the marina anyway so I could have a look around and we could all have another drink and meet some of the people who lived in the local village. Off we went to the bus stop.

After a time a clapped-out old Bedford bus came along and the driver shoved the two locals who were sitting in the front seat into the back, putting Toni and me in their place. Dikola, Mike, Douglas and a pleasantly boozy Brian were packed into the back with the two other men like sardines cooking in a pot of sweat, as the comfortable morning had quickly turned into a hot afternoon.

I was sitting up against the driver and he kept on looking at me out of the corner of his eye. Every time he changed gears he brushed against my leg.

The music on the bus was so loud, I caught the beat and would have loved to dance to the rich music. The whole heap of a bus rocked to the rhythm as the driver drove dangerously along the crowded streets. We were dropped in the village in one piece and started down a dirt path to our end destination.

The thick dust swam in and out of my new sandals, turning my feet the same red colour as the ground. I tripped on an exposed root and would have fallen had Dikola not grabbed my hand. Without exchanging words we carried on hand in hand. Anything that was in my path Dikola would move out of the way by kicking it or moving it with his rungu (club made of wood or metal) so I would not tread on anything or trip again.

He was so tall and could walk so fast, his patience with my much slower walk was endearing. We talked freely about nothing in particular. His charm captivated me and I found myself hanging on his every word. I liked his voice, I liked his smile. I liked the way his eyes sparkled every time he looked down at me. I was fascinated by the way he walked in his kanga. I had never seen a man wear so many beads and I thought that he looked wonderful. I felt him to be my majestic warrior bodyguard assigned to me personally by God.

We settled into a bar near the marina for a beer. Toni and the others sat at a table talking, while Dikola and I sat together off to the side. The bar was very touristy, having been set up for foreigners visiting the Samburu Masai site and the small zoo, as well as fisherman and yachtsmen.

I asked Toni to take my photo with Dikola. I stood by him, leaning on his chair and his arm came up to touch mine. This seemed perfectly normal to Douglas and Mike, who also came over to have their pictures taken with me. I found my thoughts distracted as I kept on looking over towards Dikola.

As we were making our way back to the disco bus stop, a lizard fell out of a tree onto my shoulder. I screamed in shock as it surprised me and I saw Dikola tense like a cat readying itself for the kill. Everybody then saw what had frightened me so and we all fell about laughing. I held Dikola's hand tighter after this and he did the same with me.

Before getting back on board a disco bus, at Brian's request, we stopped at another bar. It was a little shanty bar, dirty with wooden tables. It smelled like a sewer. There was a barred enclosure with a small opening through which drinks and money could be passed.

Both Dikola and I had small bottles of Guinness. He sat next to me, still keeping a discreet distance. He sat there scraping the label off of the bottle and I followed suit.

Toni picked up a camera urging Dikola to smile. He did, leaning over and putting his arm around my shoulder. I felt myself blush like a girl and giggled to cover up how flustered I had become. We returned to the hotel after this, saying affectionate goodbyes.

If I hide behind the frayed green chair with the wooden arms, Mum won't be able to get at me.

Besides my wood child, I haven't any toys. Fluff, the cat, recently had a litter of kittens, and these join Wood and I in play, hiding behind the green chair.

The kitten I have stolen on this occasion is black and terribly young. Fluff comes to rescue it when it utters the occasional muffled mew. I greet the mother at these times with a doggy bark, terrorising her away from her offspring.

For a time, Wood and I jolly the kitten, having formed perimeters to foil any escape. It is so soft and warm and vital. I pick it up to better feel its soft warm fur and little round belly. My wrist twists awkwardly and the kitten drops to the hard floor below. It stops moving and no longer mews.

'Oh, Wood, Oh, Wood. The kitten is broken, I broke it. It's broken.' I sigh to my baby, rocking, rocking. Wood is crying.

I crawl from my hiding place with the still body in my hand, trying not to damage it further. I run blindly to my Mother, hoping she can fix it.

'Mummy, look, look,' I cry, holding out the kitten with one hand and clutching Wood close to me with the other.

I see her face change into an angry mask as she grabs away the kitten. I watch her features then soften and fall as tears track down her cheeks, leaving behind angry red marks. She bangs into a hard chair, sobbing and clutching the dead fur between her hands.

I go back behind the green chair with Wood. There is no comfort here. For my Mother, it seems, that tear stained fur is more important than me, and deserves mourning more than I deserved peace. I try to discuss this with Wood, but Wood will no longer speak to me.

I woke up again with the feeling that Dikola was beside me in bed. I went into the toilet to cry as the feeling frightened me so much. I vomited the little I had eaten that day.

I had never been attracted to a black man before. In fact, I rarely ever found myself attracted to any man. Inter-racial relationships went against everything I believed in. I felt that this sort of relationship would be too hard on any children born of the union. I also believed that God made black for black and white for white. I never hated black people, I just hated what black and white people do to each other. Under no circumstances would I be able to accept that I was attracted to a black man. I had never been before and I certainly wasn't going to start on something so doomed now. I was a white woman, white man person and that was that.

Chapter Five

The next day I did better with keeping my emotions in check. Toni, Brian and I spent the day under a tree on Bamburi beach with a group of Samburu Masai warriors. They had met Toni and her brother on the two other occasions that she had been there. They spent their time talking and Toni busied herself keeping them in food and drink. Brian entertained everybody with jokes, once taking out his dentures, terrorising the warriors. They were on the beach to try to sell beads and spears to the tourists. They didn't sell very much and always the tourists wanted to bargain.

Dikola sat near me for most of the day, but I laughed and joked with all of the young men. Any time that Toni went off somewhere the men became more relaxed and open. Even those who didn't speak much English seemed to start to speak more freely amongst themselves.

Toni was always telling the warriors she was a true Christian woman and often preached verses of the bible to them. It didn't ring true to them and they started to ask a lot of questions. I could see that Toni had misled them in many ways. She had told them that there was no such thing as homelessness in England. I explained to them that I had been homeless at times and that some teenagers as young as thirteen can be found sleeping in cardboard boxes in freezing weather and that they would often die young from drugs and illness and the consummate danger of life on the streets.

They wanted to know about my life, or rather Dikola did. I told them I was still married but had come to Kenya to think about getting a divorce because I was so very unhappy. I explained that it was my second marriage and that I had three children, two sons from my first marriage and a daughter from my second. Dikola could not believe that I had three children because I looked so young. After a time the group began to disperse and I decided to walk along the beach for a time. Dikola decided to walk with me.

After we had walked a short distance Dikola caught hold of my hand. It didn't feel at all awkward, it seemed the most natural thing on earth. Everybody who we passed gaped at us, I suppose that we did look a bit unusual.

We walked and talked and sat in the sand like long lost friends who had just found each other after years of separation. For all of Dikola's lack of schooling he was unusually wise and perceptive. He was mostly self taught and I admired that. I found in passing various people that he could speak English, German, Swahili, Masai and a little Italian. Dikola and I were like loving kids playing in the sand, but we hid it from Toni.

Dikola asked me on that Friday afternoon if I would come to the Mtwapa disco that night, providing that he and the boys arranged it with Toni. I said that I would. They worked on Toni and she hesitated but agreed, as she had never been to Mtwapa at night. I think that she was confused as to why she had never been asked herself on her previous visits. I suppose that she was jealous. She had tried to buy them, something that I never could or would do, yet I was the one holding their attention rather than her. But she agreed, and that was the important thing.

Later in the day I started feeling very ill. I stayed in the hotel for the remainder of the afternoon, as I was vomiting so much. The time came for Dikola to pick us up in the lobby of the hotel, the others coming along as our unofficial bodyguards. I was trying very hard to feel better as I didn't want to disappoint Dikola, who I knew had been looking forward to taking me to this shanty town disco.

When he arrived he was wearing western style clothing and I was staggered to see him as they made him look so different. His long hair was hidden under a hat. His clothes were second hand and did not fit properly. Even his shoes were off some tourist at the beach. I preferred him dressed as a Masai. I loved the costumes, they made our clothes look so boring. It was sexy and he was sexy and I had never thought of a man in those terms before.

The bus that took us to the disco was a big old rattly thing built like a tank. It seemed just slightly safer than the disco bus of the day before. Dikola sat in the seat in front of me and stared out of the window as I was still feeling unwell. He looked back at me every now and then, tenderly. I remember thinking 'Oh God, this guy is in love with me'. I knew that I couldn't possibly cope with that and decided that I must find the right time to tell him that things between us couldn't possibly work as I lived so far away and already had three children and a husband who didn't make me happy, but was still a good husband.

We soon arrived at an open air disco named Pimica. Though ours were the only three white faces, I somehow did not feel out of place. Toni fidgeted and Brian headed for the bar. As soon as I sat down I needed to be sick again. Toni told Dikola and he took me by the hand, leading me outside to be sick. He would not leave my side and I was so embarrassed.

'Just leave,' I begged.

'Don't be silly, just be sick,' he replied.

I was, repeatedly. I couldn't help myself, I just heaved and heaved. Dikola held me tight, not caring about the pool of bile that was forming at our feet. His body was shaking, he was so upset. I was getting more ill by the second and was on the verge of collapse. His strong hold comforted me. It was the first time a black man had ever held me, I never wanted him to let me go.

Toni came around to check on me and tried to pull Dikola away. I was happy where I was and couldn't figure out why she was trying to make things worse by attempting to take my weight from Dikola. Maybe she felt that Dikola and I were getting too close for comfort. After all, I was a married woman and it was not a Christian thing to do or feel.

I was so ill by now that I had to be persuaded into a taxi to get me back to the hotel. Dikola sat on one side of me and Toni was on the other. Dikola held me tight to his side and Toni was trying to pull me away. I felt like the rope in a game of tug-of-war but was too shattered to resist, being unable even to keep my eyes open. I could feel that Toni was really beginning to annoy Dikola. It seemed to have passed her by that Dikola and I were already close friends. I had to have them stop the car again so that I could be sick. I was really in a bad way. Dikola shouted at Toni to allow him to help me. He held my stomach in such a fashion that it helped with the heaving. By now I was vomiting blood from all of the straining. We got to the hotel and went to the room, leaving Dikola in the lobby. This saddened me, and I urged myself to not be so silly.

Dad is out of work again, passing the time building an Airfix model of a mini. I am sitting on the floor playing with Wood. Daddy has sent Richelle to the shop. There is a loud rapping at the door. Dad tells me to answer it, as he doesn't want to leave the model.

At the door stands a kindly looking, black haired gentleman. He holds Richelle firmly and she is crying.

My dad hears the commotion and hurries to the front door to check.

'What are you doing to my daughter?' Roars my father.

'I'm so very sorry sir, but your little girl ran out in front of me.' replies the man.

My father loses his temper and hits the man, who appears to already be slightly disabled, and pushes him back up the basement steps. He then pulls Richelle across the room by her hair. Urine is running down her legs from sheer terror. His huge hands come down upon her face and body. He tears clumps of hair out of her skull. She screams for mercy.

'Stand up straight Richelle. Where does it hurt?' demands Dad. His voice is wrong. There is no compassion or concern in the question. Richelle tentatively points to the various superficial cuts and bruises caused by the car, not knowing what to expect in his reaction. He lunges for her tearing at her damaged skin, biting her like a hungry wolf. My brain is filled with frenzied screams - Richelle's, mine and Father's cannibalistic cries.

'Does it hurt now? Now?' Demands father, pinching and tearing ever more maliciously. The noises are louder and louder. I find my voice and approach the beast feeding on my sister's terror.

'Please Daddy, stop.' I pass out.

Toni was kind to me, keeping me sponged down and cool, talking to me and telling me that if it got any worse she would go ahead and call a doctor. I fell asleep and then woke up to be sick again. I suddenly felt so awful that I couldn't feel my legs or head. I had pins and needles in my arms. I asked Toni to please get some help. She was so anxious that she couldn't even remember the number for receptionist at the desk. Brian had gone out again after returning from the disco to check on us, and had locked us in. Toni was quite anxious about getting a doctor in for me.

After an hour it was all sorted and Toni had got the help I needed. As it turned out I had simply had an adverse reaction to the anti malaria drug I was taking, combined with an anti depressant that I was taking at the time.

The doctor gave me two injections to put me to rights. He said that if I had any further problems I was to have him arrange a trip back home to a hospital in England. All the following day I was in and out of sleep. Toni was good to me when I was ill and I thanked her. She even paid for the doctor as I hadn't any money. I stayed in bed for all of the next day.

Toni told me on Saturday evening that Dikola had been asking after me and I began to feel that maybe she was beginning to accept our relationship. I certainly hoped so. I didn't want for there to be any animosity between us.

I had spent most of that day in bed thinking about Mike and how it was truly over. It had to be, regardless of what the future might hold for Dikola and me. I knew that if I could feel these kinds of things for a man that there was no way I was going to give up the opportunity of a lifetime, this sort of warmth, for a loveless marriage.

Chapter Six

I saw Dikola again on Sunday afternoon. We started out being uncomfortably quiet with each other. He spoke first, saying how worried he had been about me. We then walked and talked in the surf, learning more about each other, wanting to know everything, to consume everything we could about each other. It became almost a physical craving, this need to know. The next few lazy days were spent in this manner, hand in hand on the hot sands. On Tuesday we again agreed to try to go to the disco.

When we arrived at the place in Mtwapa we sat in the bar area. Dikola went to sit next to me. Toni pulled the chair from him, telling him to find some other place to sit. We all felt terribly silly about this, not abashed at our behaviour, as perhaps Toni intended, more embarrassed by our choice of company. I didn't want a battle with her, as she was my friend, but I also couldn't see the logic in her domineering behaviour. I was beginning to tire of my position as paid companion. Dikola became quite upset with being reprimanded like a small child, particularly about something so innocent. He resented being singled out for Toni's humiliation over the other men present.

Later, as the reggae music started up I watched the black people get up to dance without hesitation. They really seemed to know how to enjoy themselves. They danced as one is supposed to at a disco, not as they do in England with everyone standing about trying to pull someone for an evening. I envied their freedom from inhibitions, their confidence.

The place was so poor, only a few old sticks of wood nailed together. Wooden tables and benches were staggered about the room and Tuska beer flowed like water. The bar looked like a prison fortress, again with the bars up to separate the staff from the customers. The floor was dangerously uneven and dusty for the dancers pounding about, but there was more happiness and solidarity in that room than in any European disco I had ever been to.

I wanted desperately to dance, but Toni kept on pulling me back. She wasn't terribly good company that night and kept on complaining and criticising everything in that wonderfully alive little ghetto disco.

Dikola approached me to ask if I would like to dance. I was so nervous getting up to dance with all of the African people. Toni and I were the only white people there that night, Brian had chosen to stay at the hotel, resting after previous excesses.

Dikola and I kept a good distance between us whilst dancing. I could see Toni shooting daggers at me with her eyes. She was making me feel incredibly uncomfortable and dirty, like I was the worst sinner of all time.

Dikola was daring to come nearer and nearer to me. It exhilarated me as much as it frightened me. As he came closer and closer to me I froze in the spot where I stood. I could not dance any more as he stood before me. For the first time in my life, the desire to make love came with an animal passion. It frightened me with its intensity and I could not seem to fully comprehend the nature of this beast that had suddenly taken over my body and soul. My abusive past seemed to be cast aside by this whole new emotion. I was a woman with sexual feelings and carnal desires. I was breathing in short gasps and I felt my face flush. I never thought that this would happen to me. I felt myself to be far too damaged for such things.

Dikola backed off when he realised how distressed his close proximity had left me. A rush of people pushed him back to me. I wanted more than anything to kiss him and for him to kiss me. In this moment all was forgotten, Toni's inexplicable jealousy, my husband's indifference and my children's confused pain all seemed to dissolve in that moment that my entire being was begging for this simple kiss.

I finally broke the gaze, feeling very confused and upset. I tried to hide all this from Dikola. He knew, but respected my feelings and the situation.

Toni was getting more and more upset by the second. Dikola was coming so close, as close as he dared. I had never seen so much love in one person's eyes. I wanted to cry, to rage against a world that would put us in this impossible and volatile situation.

Toni lost her temper and told me that we had to go as a taxi was waiting to take us back to the hotel. I didn't want to go, but knew that I hadn't enough money on me to afford to get a taxi back by myself.

As we sat waiting for the taxi to pull away from the line I could see Dikola standing there, his head hung low, his emotions high; he was shaking with the anticipation.

I felt so empty, I could not take my eyes or mind from him. I was hooked forever and knew that I would always return his feelings. We loved each other. I knew this without having ever exchanged words about it. I now had to learn to accept the fact that I was in love with a black man.

'Don't get too fond of Dikola,' preached Toni on the way home, 'you are a married woman, don't lead him to believe that all of this mess is my fault, I was not the Eve in this case.'

She warned me again to stay away from Dikola. I paid no attention. *Who was she to tell me?* I thought. I knew that she felt she had paid for me and that I was an bound servant of a sort. I wasn't having it.

I started to realise Toni's true character. I recognised that my good family friend had wanted and expected to keep my friendship and absolute loyalty and subservience in all things because she was the one holding the purse strings. I was very disappointed.

I slept well that night for the first time since meeting Dikola.

Dad hit Mum so hard that she had to have surgery on her nose. The doctors are keeping her in the hospital because she has lost so much blood.

When we get home Dad is terribly tense. He makes a dinner that neither Richelle or I like. We eat it like we enjoy it. There are butterflies in my stomach and I want desperately to grab my sister and run. Daddy is always worse when Mum is gone. Richelle is eating slowly, dragging her fork between her teeth.

'Don't eat like that, don't eat like an animal!' the monster roars.

'What Daddy? What?' asks Richelle, looking like a rabbit caught in a trap.

'Don't what me, you're an animal!' yells my father. He smacks her across the head so hard that she collapses onto the floor, trembling in a pool of her own fear induced urine.

'You dirty whore, you dirty whore,' continues my father, seeing the urine. He grabs her plate of food from the table, tossing it into the puddle.

'You want to be an animal? Get on the floor and eat like a dog. That's what you are, a dog. Woof, woof.' Richelle painfully urges herself onto her hands and knees and begins to eat the urine soaked food.

'That's better,' says my father with a malicious grin. He turns to me and the smile vanishes. 'What are you looking at? You want the same?'

I return to my food, looking neither left or right. I hear the whimpering and smell the urine wafting up from the linoleum. I feel nauseous. I dare a glance at Richelle; she has finished eating the mess on the floor.

I hear my father's voice and again stare at my food.

'Cheryl, get my favourite glass,' he commands.

It is a Carling Black Label glass with a short stem and gold rim. I am so nervous carrying it, so worried that I will drop it or that the sight of me will be enough to set him off. As I reach his big chair, shaking, I drop it, shattering it into dozens of tiny fragments at his feet.

I look at the bits of glass on the floor, breathing in short shallow gasps. He seems huge. I swallow the bile that is rising in my throat. I don't know if it is possible to survive such an infraction. I look at his face. He is smiling.

'Never mind darling. Now pick it up carefully - mind that you don't cut yourself - and get me another glass and a beer.'

The next day I waited at the beach for Dikola, pretending that I wasn't. Toni kept on teasing me, asking where Dikola could possibly be. I pretended not to notice her digs, and slid my sun glasses from the top of my head to my nose to cover the moisture that was gathering in my eyes.

By late afternoon I was very upset. I asked his friends where he was and they insisted that he was simply working on the other beach and I shouldn't worry about him. I knew that they were lying to me. I turned away from the others to be on my own. I was sick to my stomach, imagining all the reasons that might have kept him away and very lonely without him. I desperately wanted to see him, to touch him, smell him, make him smile. I broke into tears. I prayed to God to not let it all end this way, to please forgive me for all of the feelings I was having for this man. I prayed to see Dikola's face just one more time.

One of the young men came up to me, as he could see that I was very upset and trying to conceal it.

'Please, please tell me the truth about Dikola,' I begged. 'Why did Dikola not come today?'

He responded that it was not good for their culture, the things that we were feeling.

'But,' he said, 'there is something kind in your eyes, and so I will tell you. Dikola did not come today because of you. He is very upset. He does not want to spoil your friendship with Toni. He can see that she is jealous. He does not want to make problems for you, he loves you too much. He knows that you have a life in England and he has nothing to offer you because he is so poor. It is much better for him to never see your face again. He says that he will always love you, despite all of this. He is going home to Samburu forever because he knows that he will never find someone like you again. He is going home to look after the cattle.'

I was so shocked I could not speak. The Masai shook my hand, as it was nearing six o'clock and all natives have to have left the beach by this time. My feelings were so mixed, I was very happy yet almost unbearably sad.

I broke into a run and found myself sprinting after the tall warrior in the dusky light.

'Please tell Dikola for me that I would like very much to see him. Tell him I must see him. Ask him to come to me tomorrow. I will wait for him on this beach.'

'Yes,' said his friend, and he disappeared.

Chapter Seven

That night I never even went to bed. I stayed up all night in the lobby with a drink, but not getting drunk. I felt very sorrowful and restless, as if I had just been told of a loved one's passing. I was grieving and frightened. I didn't know how to deal with my feelings at all well.

Noon came around the next day and I had given up any pretence of pride. I wanted only Dikola. I came up to any friend of his that appeared on the beach, begging for his location.

'He will be here,' they all promised, confused at my very obvious desperation.

Toni mocked me, teasing that I was only happy with Dikola. She had become so sarcastic. Unable to face other people any longer, I left to swim in the sea.

I swam out to a glass bottomed boat moored close to the shore, clinging to it, sobbing, my tears mixing with the salty water. I had a good cry and made my way to shore to reluctantly accept the fresh disappointment that was sure to be awaiting me onshore.

When I reached the beach, I looked up and met Dikola's eyes from only a short distance. He looked very tired and worse for wear. I smiled at him, not wanting to give too much away. He looked edgy, like he could run in either direction, into my arms or out of my life.

I looked around, neither Toni nor Brian were anywhere to be seen. Without words and with about ten of his friends looking on, Dikola and I silently approached each other and joined hands. We walked down the beach and then off a slip path. We sat on a large wooden box at the back of the hotel in which we were staying. We said nothing, just enjoying the presence of the other, memorising each other with our eyes. I reached out my hand, touching the back of his neck.

He shuddered and let out a small yip, an animal wanting to mate. 'Can you feel it?' he asked, 'can you feel the feeling that I am feeling?' A basic natural instinct to make love. It took over all of my senses and was the best thing that I had ever felt in my life.

'Yes, yes, I feel it,' I whispered back. I was shocked by my own honesty. I was so used to hiding my feelings or just pretending, keeping everybody else happy. This was so different. It was something I had never known.

As we touched each other lightly we could hardly handle the feelings which alienated our very bodies. We had to catch our breath and were a little sheepish about the overwhelming feelings that existed between us. I felt that I was dreaming. I thought I was crazy.

I asked him if he had ever believed before that such feelings could exist between two people.

'No,' he said 'I thought that love was only something that others talk and pretend about. I did not think I would have feelings such as this. Please do not make fun of me. I am a poor black man. I don't know what to do.'

I thought to myself that he was rich, rich in many ways that I hadn't ever come across in anybody before.

'I missed you yesterday,' I told him, 'why did you not come?'

He told me what his friend had told me the day before and I was moved to the brink of tears. We were in love. This was something so new to me. How was I to cope with this? How could I ever find the strength to leave Dikola when the time came?

We started walking along again, looking for a more private spot where we would not be observed. We came to a log in some bush land, shielded from everybody.

We sat close, talking but not touching. If ever we brushed against each other he made the little animal noise again. He seemed so confused as to what to do with this white flesh beside him.

I was concerned, because I knew that those of his tribe did not use kissing as part of their love making rituals. If I kissed him, would he leave? Would he be insulted? I didn't want to lose him, didn't want to lose this precious time together, this moment.

I put my face as close to his as I could. I had seen some tourists greet him with a friendly peck, so I knew that he must have some idea. I did the same. I gently kissed his face as he looked at me shyly. He returned my kisses until finally our mouths met and we kissed. We stayed together for hours. We were not to be separated. We felt completely stranded and cut off from the world and liked it that way. Worlds apart had come together.

We have our first real Christmas tree. It is covered with small chocolates wrapped in coloured paper. We are young enough to believe in Father Christmas and the tree seems like a gift from God.

Richelle and I sit before the tree feasting our eyes as our stomachs growl for the brightly wrapped sweets. Our father comes into the room and, noting our greedy faces, smiles and tells us that we can have some sweets off the tree. It is Christmas Eve, after all.

The little packets are beautiful; red, blue and green with delicate gold twine binding them to the tree. Richelle and I both take a very few of these gilded packets down, unwrapping them slowly, savouring the luxury of Dad's new found generosity. The moment ends as he leaps back through the door of the kitchen.

'You pigs, you pigs, you pigs, you greedy pigs!' he roars as spittle flies from his mouth.

'You ate all of the chocolates and you didn't save me one. Not even one!' I look up at our tree, still shimmering with its burden of small chocolate sweets.

'Oh Daddy, we're so sorry,' I say as I have learned to do. 'It's her, she's the little pig, look at her!' he rages, pointing at my whimpering sibling.' Look how fat she is.'

He pulls her off the sofa by her hair. Richelle is screaming frantically not realising, as I did, that this to him is an added incentive; the red cape in front of a charging bull. I will her to stop. I want to tell her not to cry or scream, what it does to him. He can't ever make me scream.

Richelle is crying and shaking with fear as her bladder empties onto the floor in front of the tree. He continues to punch and slap her, screaming abuse.

'Please stop Daddy,' Richelle begs through her tears 'I'm a good girl, I'm a good girl.'

'No you're not. You're a whore, a prostitute. You're shit! Do you hear me? You're shit. What are you? What are you?'

'I'm shit, Daddy, I'm shit.'

'To bed, both of you. Father Christmas will not be coming tomorrow.'

Creeping out the following morning it seems that nothing happened, except for a prominent bruise painted on Richelle's face. We open our gifts with as much feigned enthusiasm as possible, playing the part for Mum and Dad.

Richelle has a cold and can't seem to stop coughing. Daddy makes her a drink to try and knock it out of her: Brandy, sugar, honey, menthol and hot water. It is a nasty brew and there is a lot of it. Richelle can't drink it all so I start taking swigs of it for her whenever Daddy's back is turned. We have nearly finished the vile liquid when Dad turns and catches us.

My father throws himself at Richelle, screaming that she has forced me to drink it, forces her mouth open and pours the remainder of it down her. Richelle's fear, coupled with the warm cloying liquid, is too much for her and she vomits all over my father.

'You fucking pig!' He spits into her face, already wet with tears. She has wet herself again and he begins beating her like never before. He is crazed, a rabid dog.

'Please, Daddy, Please,' begs Richelle. 'It's Christmas Day.'

'I don't care if it's bloody Chinese Day,' comes his reply.

Something snaps in Mum. With a strangled scream she leaps at my father, a kitten attacking an outsized Alsatian dog.

'Leave her alone,' she pleaded, 'leave her alone!'

Dad is expecting the attack and falls as Mum hurls herself at him. He recovers quickly and smashes her face with his large, meaty fist.

The doorbell rings.

I rush to the door, frantic to see whoever it was, praying that it would be somebody, anybody who could do something to diffuse the situation. I open the door to the police.

A policewoman takes my sister and I aside to comfort and question us. Richelle and I tell her nothing and so we stayed.

If we left, who would protect Mum? After all, what are kids for?

Dikola had to leave me because the local law did not permit him to hang about after dark. Already the blanket of night was descending over the bush when he saw me into the hotel, leaving quickly to avoid the authorities.

When I returned I found that Toni had called a search party after me. She had the entire place mobilised, as if I was days late instead of it being only six-thirty. I was told that she had been looking for me since around two.

She said that she knew I had been out with Dikola. She said that since she had been the one to bring me to Kenya in the first place I should be at her beck and call. If I spent one moment more with Dikola she purported that she would put me on the next plane out of there. This was our tenth day, we had eleven more to go.

She decided that we could no longer be friends because I was treating her so badly. She did not realise that everybody else saw it the other way around. I stayed silent.

She tried so hard to get a reaction, going so far as to say that she would tell Mike about my trampy behaviour with Dikola. I told her to go ahead, as there was nothing left in my relationship with Mike that could be salvaged. I couldn't live as a nun anymore. I was going to grab life by the balls and run with it, Mike be damned. He had taken his status in my life for granted for far too long. Dikola or no, the marriage was dead. It had been the rotting elephant in the middle of the room for far too long. I wanted to bury it. I would go home and start divorce proceedings.

For the first time in my life I was really taking a good look at myself. I wanted to find what I really liked and what I didn't like. What I want and how to get it. Will I like it when I get there?

Toni told me to do as I wished. I nodded at her and walked away, leaving her to look after the remaining tatters of her search party.

It didn't take Toni long to start talking to me again. Her main purpose was to tell me what a horrible monster Dikola was, a complete change from the fine Christian boy she had been painting up to this point, but at least she was talking.

I took little notice of her pettiness. She had only been there on two other occasions, once for two weeks and the other for three, yet she could stand there and claim to be an authority on the life, loves and habits of all of the Samburu tribe. She said that she had been going there and had known Dikola for years. I suggested that she check her passport and give her imaginative brain a rest.

The next day I asked Dikola to take me in to the Mombasa city centre to buy Toni a thank you gift for my holiday to Kenya.

She was not pleased to hear this and tried to insist I take someone, anyone, besides Dikola. She tried to gather more people around her to be invited, and all of Dikola's friends were giving him very funny looks.

I told her that I was going with Dikola and that was that. She left in a huff and refused to speak to me. I wondered at the true nature of her problem. She began to spread stories amongst all of Dikola's friends about me. In the end I spat in the sand in the place she was sitting and walked away. She cooled it a bit after this.

Daniel spent our days talking, kissing and cuddling with each other on the beach. Toni happened upon us on one occasion, causing quite a fuss, but she had her big say earlier in the week and now had more interesting things to concern herself with.

Chapter Eight

Dikola and I began meeting more and more Westerners during the time that we spent together, often with the other warriors.

Two girls had been seeing the group of us on the beach quite frequently and were very curious about us. Finally one of them approached and started to speak to me in an Irish accent. It was funny hearing such an accent so far from home. I was used to it, having an Irish stepfather, and could understand what she was saying, but the warriors couldn't work it out at all and thought that she might even have been speaking a different language.

I tried to explain Northern Ireland to them in geographic terms, but it was fruitless without a map and we all ended up laughing.

The girl, Emily, came back with her funny accent to ask us what we were laughing at, and it made us laugh ever harder.

We started talking and she appeared to be very pleasant company. She was travelling with her twin sister and her family, acting as a baby-sitter for the young children as the parents were there for business.

She found herself gradually being sucked into the group and we were glad to have the company. She was lonely in Kenya, having only her sister's family for company, her British boyfriend being at home. She got on well with all of us and became great friends with Brian, Toni's brother. They were both funny and made all the rest of us laugh. She had never spent time with the Masai, though she had spent a lot of time in Kenya. She found the experience to be a nice surprise for her.

Emily was one of those girls who never seemed to have any luck when it came to men. After hearing her stories about previous relationships, I can't say that what happened with her next was too much of a surprise.

In the third week, Dikola invited me into his home and into his world. It was a small mud hut, resembling a hollowed out Oxo cube.

I couldn't comprehend how these people could survive such conditions, I felt sure that no western person would ever be able to etch out any kind of existence under such circumstances, much less the rich life and culture that was present amongst Dikola and all of his peers.

I spent twenty four hours in one of these huts. In this time I had no food and only three cokes to drink. Dikola told me that he often went up to five days without food and only a single drink a day. I was horrified at this. My brief time of purgatory was enough for me to truly begin to understand what these people must go through from day to day, but still the idea of five days without nourishment was beyond my understanding.

Dikola saw my reaction written on my face and said, 'What is wrong Cheryl? This, which is so terrible to you, is perfectly normal for us.'

I would look around the hut with its crusty mud walls and be thankful for my circumstances. Cracks zigzagged through the mud, letting in sunlight. The roof was made of dry rush, weaved together like a thatched cottage. It was ingeniously done.

Rats and newts ran across the floor and the roof. Black snakes hung down from the beams.

My bed for this trial run was a broken down cardboard box. Cobwebs climbed the wooden beams, fat spiders hung down, nibbling at prey or waiting for more. Even the spiders ate more in this country than the men.

I have begun to walk in my sleep. Sometimes when I walk I end up next door at my friend Sally's house. Usually her mother comforts my night terrors and tucks me in top and tail in my friend's bed. Other times she carries me back home and tucks me quietly into my own bed.

Mum has been having me sleep in her bed so that she will not have to sleep with Dad. Last night in my sleep I left her bed and walked to Sally's. I wake up in her bed with stomach cramps and am returned to my own bed to rest.

My father comes to my room before he leaves the flat for the day, asking me where my stomach hurts. I have only my pyjama top on and I point to a spot just to the left of my right hipbone.

'Here?' he asks, pointing again to the spot. I nod in confirmation. He slams his big fist into the spot, winding me.

'There, it hurts now, doesn't it?' he chortles. I begin to cry, being careful to do so quietly.

'Fine,' he says, 'if you are going to stay home today, you will do all of the hoovering. If it is not done properly by the time I get home then you will repeat it continuously until it is.' With this he leaves. My tired mind begs him to never come back.

My Mum comes into the room before she leaves for work. 'Why didn't you come to my bed last night?' She hisses. 'I had to sleep with your father.'

'I'm sorry Mum, I fell asleep.'

'Oh God. Just do what your father asked.'

I cry after she leaves. I feel ghastly but am afraid of the consequences if I don't do what has been instructed. I hoover the front hall and Mum's and Dad's room three times.

Whilst hoovering the front room I bump against the bookshelf, knocking one of the volumes to the floor. I pick up the book and some pictures slip from between the pages, onto the floor. Some of the pictures are of my mother, naked, undulating in some kind of bizarre dance. Other pictures involve my mother posing with other women, some of whom I recognise as being her friends. The last picture is of a man with scabs covering his body from chest to knees, his penis having been completely eaten away.

I run from the room and vomit. I neither understand nor like this adult world that keeps on thrusting itself beneath my nose.

In this place the native's only hope for survival was to find a friendly tourist who might buy them dinner or pick up a few bracelets that some poor woman had spent ages working on.

Their most desperate ploy was to send the young boys out to prostitute themselves for old women. It seemed as though most of the men who were driven to such extremes were married with children. Having to feed their families they would sleep with these old hags. It was this or starvation. I was told that afterwards they usually vomit.

Still, I wanted so much to be a part of Dikola's world, to get under the surface, to know everything, I was grateful even for this. We had become so vital to each other in such a short period of time, I had no idea how I would survive the separation.

There was a friend of Dikola's, Douglas, who took quite a shine to Emily, the Irish girl, and trusted me enough to tell me and ask me to gently let the cat out of the bag. There was a lot of gossip at the time about everybody. It seemed that everyone wanted what Dikola and I had.

And for a while it worked. Emily was to stay in Mombasa for some months and it seemed natural for the two to get together. Watching them fall in love was like something out of a movie. They would splash in the water for hours like lovers in a lost paradise.

Emily and Douglas understood each other about as much as a zebra understands a giraffe and after all has been said, I think it is fair to assume that the relationship was largely made up of physical attraction. They liked the danger of a high risk relationship, but had about as much a chance of surviving it as you or I might have surviving a nuclear holocaust. The feelings went deep but the understanding between the two was only shallow.

Emily was constantly in search of happiness and made no bones about it. She nursed all mistakes with a shrug of the shoulder and went on to the next adventure. If there was a chance of something happening to her there was no way she was going to pass it by. I wished her luck before it was my time to leave.

The last day came. My feelings were scattered all over the place. I finally closed myself to them, they were too intense. I tried to see everything with a sense of humour, to lighten the things that were weighing so heavily on my heart.

A group of us had some beers in one of the beach bars. Dikola was with us, deathly quiet. He got up and left us, going over to sit one hundred yards away from the group, his face to the wall. I tried to pretend I hadn't noticed, but my attention was on him always. The others started making fun of me, saying I was love sick. Dikola caught my eye and beckoned me over. I was glad to go to his side.

'Cheryl,' he began, 'in all of my life, with all my heart I know I will never find one like you again. I will see your face in my mind forever. Please don't forget about me when you go home. I know you have your own life there, your children, Mike, but please, I beg you from my heart, don't ever forget me. I will never forget you, you are in my heart.' He spat lightly on his hand.

He continued, 'In all of my days I have never met so kind a person as you. You have been a good friend to Toni, but if you come back to Kenya again, do not do so on Toni's money. Next time I want you to be able to walk and talk and feel as you want to without being Toni's prisoner. You deserve better than this. Be free from her and I will wait forever for your return.'

I was speechless. Such a wise head on such young shoulders. I started crying, the emotions I had been trying to ignore burst through the brittle barriers I had been attempting to build up against this man and this place and most of all myself.

He begged me not to cry, wiping away my flood of tears with his hands. I hadn't felt such grief since being abandoned by my mother in the children's home with my sister. I was gutted. Never had anybody spoken to me so tenderly. I had come all the way to Africa to find this wonderful man and now fate was taking away the gift which had been given so freely.

Four o'clock came and it was time to board the coach home. I tried to put myself on an emotional high again to cope with the goodbye. The group of Masai whom we has spent to much time with lined up outside the coach to see us off. We all said our goodbyes, tearfully. I was the only one not on the coach and the others waited for me to board. I stood there staring up at Dikola's sad brown eyes. I held him gently and we looked at each other with a passion diffused only by the tears curtaining our eyes.

'I think you are beautiful,' I breathed at him.

'I love you,' he whispered back.

I boarded the bus. The coach started out of the hotel drive. 'Oh look, Cheryl,' said Toni, 'look at Dikola, you've broken his heart. He's crying his eyes out. I told you not to let him grow fond of you, poor little thing.'

I watched him, his head hung low in grief. I went numb with my own distress and had to put on a stalwart front to hide all that I was feeling about the past three weeks. I would cry later.

The flight went by so quickly as I thought of Dikola, I could hardly believe it when we touched English soil, ten hours from the new life that I had found.

When I opened the front door of my pretty little semi in Newport it seemed entirely too clean, in contrast to my thoughts. I didn't want to stay there, I wanted to turn around and run out, swim back to Africa if I had to.

Mike came to greet me, making a terrible fuss.

I just stood there watching him as I would a stranger. I felt so sorry for him, trying so hard to keep everybody happy, to no avail. It was sad for me to realise that pity was the last emotion I had to apply to this funny, boring little man I had married. I didn't find him attractive, and wondered why I had ever thought that it would be a good idea to allow him into my life. I realised I had found more joy in my three weeks with Dikola than in the entire six years I had been married to Mike.

I had come to accept that the situation with Mike was no longer tolerable. I knew that this would hurt the children enormously, and only hoped I could make the time less painful for them.

The children were happy to see me. They had come to appreciate me in this and my previous absences. Perhaps they were just frightened I would defect again. This possibility saddened and sobered me.

'Did you get my fax at the hotel?' asked Mike 'It told you that we all loved and missed you.'

I told him that I hadn't, but was uninterested in the whole thing. I wanted to be with my children. I wanted to look at my situation now that I was back on my home turf. I needed time to make sense of the last three weeks from where I was standing right at this very moment. I needed schemes and solutions, and time to mourn.

Mike started telling me that everything was alright now and perhaps now we could really try to make an honest go at the marriage. He begged for one last chance. He said that in the time I was away he had time to think and he thought he could see what he had been doing wrong. I smiled at him and summoned the children to my room to help me unpack and see all of the goodies I had brought for them.

Chapter Nine

I found it very difficult to settle into any kind of life again with Mike. I left the house at any excuse. Mike would kiss me on the cheek as I would pass and I would only smile sadly and give him a pat on the hand at most. I felt awful about how I was treating him, but didn't feel the truth behind my melancholia would make him much happier. I wanted to leave it until I had everything straight in my head.

Mike and I had long ago given up sleeping in the same bed. Sex was a far away memory. Really, it was a miracle we ever had Chloie. I thought always of Dikola as I turned off the lights for sleep.

I began slowly to tell Mike and the children about Dikola. I had an eight by ten framed picture of him by the bed. But still, I couldn't share with them my feelings for him. Not yet.

I asked Mike for a divorce again, but still he either didn't or wouldn't hear me. I suppose maybe he was still in love with me and was simply too hesitant to say what he felt. He was so timid, so worried about saying the wrong thing. I think he finally decided not to say anything for fear that it would be the wrong thing.

I called Dikola after only a few days. I heard his voice on the line and couldn't say a thing. It was so good to hear him and imagine myself there with him. I was longing for him desperately, wishing that we had made love. I had held back from consummating our relationship because I wanted to be really sure of Dikola. I was terrified that he might simply see me as a ticket to freedom.

I knew if we slept together I would never be able to simply leave it in the past. I was also terribly concerned about the possibility of getting an STD. Dikola told me his sexual experiences had been limited, but it still worried me.

At home I found myself becoming more and more irritable with the children and Mike. Everything seemed to either set me off or get me down. The more time that went by, the more I felt Dikola's absence. It was not a Polaroid memory, fading after time, it was a living vital thing, an energy built between two people, so viable it could never fade. I became a terror to live with. I wanted Dikola so much. I felt lost once again, Dikola my only beacon on a lonely plain.

I got a letter from Dikola shortly after my return. Reading it, I broke into tears, collapsing onto the floor of the bedroom I had once shared with my husband. Dikola's letter read:

'Remember what I said on the beach to you that last day. I meant it. I love you in my heart. Not because you are white and have money. I know that you don't have your own money, Toni was always telling me about you. I love you forever and ever. I can only pray that God will bring you back to me one day soon. I am a poor black man with no power in this life. I know that it is wrong for me to love you. I can't help that I love you so much. God forgive me.'

The letter left me pining all the more. I wanted desperately to go back to see him, if only for a moment, but I had not the money to carry out such a wish. Toni telephoned the next day asking if I would like to go to Kenya for two weeks in March. I was so glad to be thrown this lifeline I forgot all of Dikola's warnings and gladly accepted her invitation. I needed to know if this was the real thing or just a way to escape poor Mike and the hackneyed life we had with each other.

I told Mike we could no longer afford to run the car now that we had both been out of work for so long, and must sell it. We got one thousand pounds for it, which we put in the bank and I earmarked for Kenya. I also arranged for a five hundred pound loan to be put on hold at the bank for me. I didn't want to come home at the same time as Toni. If this was the real thing there was no way I was going to give it up after only another two week visit. I was going to experience this man's life if it was the last thing I ever did.

I kept all of my plans to myself. It was my secret and it helped me to retain my sanity while I was wishing for my life back and waiting to get to Kenya and Dikola.

Mike was not at all happy about me going off to Kenya again. In fact, he was very angry, both with me and with Toni. He then realised that there was nothing that he could say to make me stay, and gave in. I can only imagine what that cost him.

The children were also very distraught at my leaving again so soon. They didn't understand why I needed to create this world away from them. I told them about Dikola at this time. I needed them to understand. I needed them to know why it was so important that I go back to see this man. They still didn't understand, but at least they had an explanation.

Toni started playing games with me, withdrawing her offer and then giving it again, playing on my emotions, seeing just how far she could push me and how much gratitude she could summon. She was up and down like a yo yo, making all of her feelings apparent.

I started to do some hairdressing from home to make some extra money. I gathered together things I could carry over as gifts; second hand children's clothes, cutting tools, sewing utensils, buttons, toys, even a blanket.

The day of departure came. I had not seen Dikola for eight weeks. It seemed a lifetime. For the first time that I can remember, I was really looking forward to something.

Mike chose not to see me off.

As we pulled into the Bamburi Beach Hotel, Dikola and Luria were standing on the tarmac waiting for us. We got out of the tourist coach and I could see that Dikola was visibly shaking with emotion. His only greeting was a very nervous smile and handshake. He tried to kiss me on the mouth, but I turned to let him kiss me on the cheek instead. I did not want to expose my feelings so soon. I was already feeling very vulnerable.

We sat in the arrival lounge just looking at each other. Dikola was being very serious. It all had an unreal quality, us being together again. It felt dreamlike and there was a funny buzzing in my head from the heat, excitement and emotional exhaustion.

Brian had come with us again and sat with Luria and Toni, who was over in another portion of the lounge, showering Luria with gifts that she had bought him of clothing and gold. I pitied her feeling the best she had to offer was what she owned rather than what she was. I pitied her for being right.

Later in the day we went to Mtwapa to the area that everyone lived in who worked the beaches of Mombasa selling the beaded necklaces, bracelets, watchstraps and the other brightly coloured sundries. They worked so hard for so little. They were allowed by law to sell their goods only between nine and five. If they were caught on the beach after this time they could be arrested. If they did not buy the beach trading license, this was also grounds for imprisonment.

The Samburu men would club together if one was taken for one reason or another. They would get their companion out as soon as they could. I had helped to get one warrior released. He was stuck in a vile concrete cubical, covered with urine and faeces. Prisoners were left to lie for hours in the blackness, as there were no windows and a solid door. There was no furniture. They were fed only once a day on a white cake-like substance called sima that tastes, at best, like soggy rice.

The man I aided was in for not having a beach licence and for being there after six o'clock. They wanted 6,000,000 KS, about seventy pounds, to get him out. Business had been so bad on the beach that the others could not raise enough money for his release. We managed to just get together the balance of the money and get him out.

In the small hours of the morning I hear a wailing sound coming up from the scullery yard. I have never heard a noise quite so frightening. I try to squeeze my eyes shut and burrow under the covers into a quiet place, but this is not to be.

My eyes have become accustomed to the dark. The door is ajar. I decide to see what sort of creature is keening so painfully. I step out into the dark hallway; the residence of so many fearful things for me, a small child, listening to painful cries in the pre-dawn hours.

I slowly make my way to the scullery and the source of the frightening noises. The door is ajar and I creep towards the lighted crack. Through the slit I can see the sweating figure of my mother, kneeling on hands and knees in a pool of bright red blood. She is naked from the waist down and crying horribly and hopelessly. I stay in my place, terrified to move in either direction.

Mum never sees me standing there, in that doorway watching her, as she had become blind to all but the incredible pain in the centre of her being. She lets out a final almighty scream as even more blood spurts from her womb.

She sits down hard upon the floor, grabbing up what appears to be a small plastic doll from the gore in the centre of the kitchen.

'Oh, my baby, my baby,' she croons in a monotone voice through her tears. 'My baby, my baby.'

I feel a hand on my shoulder and look up to see my nan standing above me. I haven't heard her approach, so intent am I on the activities in the kitchen. She roughly orders me to my room. I walk slowly, listening to the voices in the kitchen. Mummy's voice follows me sobbing 'Look Mum, look what I have done, I have murdered. I am a murderess, a murderess. My son. My little boy.' Nan begs her to silence so she won't scare us children.

The day the Samburu prisoner was released he looked horrible. He was far thinner than he had been before being locked away. His eyes were glassy and fixed like those of a mad man. He swayed from side to side and his body was a mass of sores and boils. He had been there for ten weeks.

At the same time they released a boy of the age of seventeen. He looked about thirty. His head had been shaven and was nicked and cut in various places where they had been clumsy with the razor. For three months he had suffered in that dank cell.

That evening I talked with Dikola about making love. I was so afraid of all the disease and filth that I saw around me. I asked him if he would be willing to go to hospital to get the tests done for all of the various STDs that were about. He was not offended or upset and we went in the next day.

We went to the hospital in Mombasa to have the tests done. It cost sixteen pounds for each of us, a lot of money for a Kenyan. We were to come back after two days for the results.

I was so nervous waiting in the hospital for the results that day. We were both clean. In my relief I threw my arms around Dikola and cried, I had just about convinced myself that this would be it, the thing to destroy our happiness.

I was worried about making love with Dikola as I had been celibate for so long. He was also anxious as I was his first real girlfriend and, having been married twice, had more experience than him.

I told Dikola that if we made love I would not be going home with Toni on the thirty first of that month. I wanted to stay and learn everything that I could about Dikola and his life, his corner of the planet. I had enough to live rough for about two months. I would write to Mike and tell him that I was in love with another man and there was no future for the two of us.

The day after we got our results Dikola came to meet me Toni and I at the hotel. We kissed and played in the sand like the little children. We always were together. I was wearing a red kanga that I had bought on that first day on the beach for only three pounds. It was the same kanga I spread on the floor of huts to keep clean and on beaches to keep the sand away. It had shaded me from the sun and shielded me from others as a curtain. We made love on it for the first time that night.

When we were playing on the beach that day Dikola wrapped another Kanga around me and asked me to come with him to Mtwapa. I agreed, nervous as I understood the implications of what he was asking.

We boarded the bus with a dozen or so other people. The driver couldn't take his eyes off of us. He had an infectious laugh and was saying 'Oh my deary lord, I see here too much love, too much love.' Soon the whole bus was in fits of laughter, particularly when the conductor began to strut up and down the aisle singing a very naughty song. We were so happy. When we got off the bus, cheers could be heard from inside as it pulled away.

We booked ourselves into a cheap room, only a pound for a couple of hours. It was a windowless grey cell with a wooden framed bed and a single bulb. There was a small wooden table with clean sheets folded onto it and a clean, tattered towel. For an extra ten pence we could have a bucket of cold water. It was seedy, to say the least, and maybe not the ideal place for making love, but for us it was perfect.

Dikola could see that I was terrified. I was afraid that my feelings might be some passing illusion, something I was reaching for out of need rather than because of any real emotion.

Dikola was eyeing me, seeing if I would do something first, as out of the two of us I was the more experienced. I panicked as the situation suddenly became entirely too real and claustrophobic. I couldn't go through with it. What if it was awful, what if it added only more weight to my unhappiness. I couldn't bear another disappointment, more pain. I ran to open the door.

Dikola caught me by the shoulder and turned me around to face him. He held the door closed with his right hand and locked it with his left. I was trapped between him and the door. He kissed me hard on the mouth, breathing in short gasps. His intensity was exhilarating and frightening. His left hand shot up and deftly untied the knot of my blood red kanga. He threw it onto the bed. I was wearing only my swimming costume and sandals.

Dikola stopped, looking at me, soaking in every bit of me. He came forward and took my hands, sitting me gently on the edge of the bed. He removed my shoes, tenderly dusting off the day's walking. He leaned me gently back on my kanga, leaving me to deal with my swimming costume. I would only be as vulnerable as I was ready to be.

He lay next to me. He was naked under his kanga and beads. Slowly, he undid the knot and threw aside the bit of fabric. He began to take off his beads, bit by bit, keeping my eyes locked in his gaze. I barely breathed.

He leaned forward and kissed me, at first slowly and then with growing intensity. I felt moisture on our faces and realised we were both crying.

We made love five times in those first three hours in that tiny grey cell.

Then that night in a beach shack we paid ten pence for our privacy in an old hut. We left our kangas on to ensure it. Our love making became stronger and stronger after this as we became more familiar with each other's bodies. We made love often and well.

Chapter Ten

My daylight hours were spent getting to know the people of the area, particularly the children. Even the most basic medical attention was unavailable to the poorer Kenyans. I would carry a first-aid kit with me and was always cleaning cuts and putting plasters on the children who would queue for attention. I had to stretch my antiseptic a long way to ensure that all of the children got the medical attention they needed.

I would coax them over for treatment with the bags of sweets I had smuggled over. They were always very good about sharing them.

I grew very fond of one family in particular, relatives of Dikola's. Their names were Kakasi and Elizabeth Lekimenju and they had three children, Emily, Suzanne and Moses. They lived in a concrete room, ten feet by seven. The only modern device was a camp Calor gas ring.

The room was full of dust and dirt and crawling cockroaches. I would see them dropping off of the clothes hung out for drying, crawling up people's kangas, burrowing in the beds and creeping across the food. I dreaded their home as much as I anticipated the company of the Lekimenju's.

They were a lovely family. The eldest daughter, Suzanne, would follow her Mum about the house, doing all she could in her rag dress and bare feet. The mother was a placid person, who had a calm acceptance of all around her. She was always in pain and I gave her as many painkillers as I could. I hope one day to help Kakasi send Moses to school, forty pounds a year.

The thirty-first of Marchcame, the day of departure. After all I had seen and done, I simply couldn't get on that plane with Toni. I wanted to learn more, feel more, do more for all of these people who had so quickly become a part of my life. Most of all I wanted to stay with Dikola and be a part of his life. I needed to be with him to touch, feel, smell, kiss him. I wanted to give him a rest from the misery he had to survive from day to day. I needed to stay where I felt most alive.

Toni was very upset when she left in only the company of her brother. I was staying and she, with all of her money, was on a plane home. I think a large portion of her resentment was based on the idea that she could be favoured because of her finances, yet I found myself staying, having nothing to offer besides myself. She told me that I was incredibly selfish and my two trips over had been an obscene waste of her money. She hated thinking of what she was going to tell Mike. I told her that I had already written to him. He knew it was over.

I boarded the bus with Toni to say goodbye. The bus driver began to pull away. Horrified I screamed for him to stop. Toni gazed up at me, shocked. I don't think that she really believed I would stay until that moment.

I was now alone in Kenya, Dikola my primary anchor. We got a taxi to Mtwapa after collecting my cases from one of Dikola's friends on the beach. We went to a small guest house where he had already booked a room and spent two nights in one of it's large, grey rooms, with only a slowly spinning ceiling fan and a double bed with a single sheet on it. The most luxurious item in the room was Dikola's radio. He had a few poor quality tapes which we played, as the only three radio stations that came in gave very inferior reception, two in Swahili and one in English.

The standards are so different in Kenya to what they are in England. You don't hear about anything going on in the outside world. Freedom of speech is a concept of western society and strictly forbidden. Little information at all is given to the people, in the hopes that meagre knowledge will result in a lack of hope and a repression of rebellion. The snippets of news that we got on the radio were minor and largely irrelevant to the people who heard them. When living in poverty, what of concern is the world beyond your home anyway?

The owner of the house in which we were staying got to know us and learned that I was trying to stay in the country for as long as possible. He moved Dikola and me into a more private room, away from the bar. They installed a wardrobe and gave me the key, saying that I could lock all of my things inside safely. They added a settee and two chairs and tables. The room was painted horrid shades of green and yellow. The window was a hole cut in the wall with iron bars and green mesh net. We had a single bulb in the wall and one electrical socket. To Dikola it was very luxurious and we were very grateful for our treatment.

We cleaned it up as best we could. We picked up the mattress to dust it off and clean it up a bit and found a collection of used condoms stuck to the slats of the bed. Dikola moved to remove the mess and I yelled at him to stop, worried that they might be diseased. I got him tissues and some of the disposable rubber gloves I had brought with me. I seemed to be going through these so rapidly. I made him wash his

Dikola and I on the beachfront in Cowes, Isle of Wight.

Dikola holding his first snow on our honeymoon in Scotland.

Dikola and I in his homeland during my second trip.

Chloie's fourth birthday,
three weeks prior to returning to Kenya to get Dikola.

Dikola's first meeting with my sister Richelle
and her five daughters.

Heather, Dikola and Neil on the beach during my third trip.

Dikola after having his hair plaited in traditional Masai style.

From left: Douglas, Cheryl, Mike and Dikola.

A group of Masai Warriors in traditional dress.

Dikola and I with his mother and father.

hands repeatedly afterwards. All this for only two pounds a night.

As we began to settle into a routine together, some of Dikola's friends came in to see us. They reported that Mike had been frantically trying to reach me by telephone in the town centre of Mtwapa, located in the Ngao cafe. The men told us that we were expected at the phone at eight o'clock to receive another call. They said that they would come to our room to escort us, as it would be dark by six thirty and it would be dangerous to be out alone.

They arrived for us at seven. All six of them were in full warrior dress with clubs in their hands and knives at their sides. Because of years of training they could see things in the dark that I couldn't and would able to be able to pick out any danger. There were three to the front of me and three at the back, with Dikola at my side. I felt very honoured getting this attention as Toni had told me that the Samburu did not like what Dikola and I were doing. This was not dislike, they were taking care of me as they always did.

On another occasion, when Toni was still around, she stranded me in the middle of the village after dark when I was running a high fever. It seemed that everybody had disappeared, but I knew that there was a very strong criminal element about that had only to find me. I had nothing valuable on me, but this, I knew, would not prevent me from being a victim.

A few yards away I noticed a very tall, well built warrior had appeared, as if from nowhere. He stood silently in the middle of the street holding a lion spear. He was watching me, motionless. I steadily returned his gaze.

Finally I smiled nervously saying, in English, that I was with Dikola. He did not seem to understand what I said. I tried again in Maa, '*Lesere Dikola*.' Still he stared.

'*Supa il-murran*', I said, 'Hello Warrior.'

Finally he laughed, a rich noise from deep down in his chest. He turned me and began to push forward. I knew that I had no choice but to follow his lead, but was not afraid. We walked for nearly an hour before coming to a road.

'*E motokaa*,' he said, meaning motorcar.

I shook my head and pointed to an approaching bus, labelled for the hotel. I turned out my pockets to show I had no money.

He looked at me sadly and then fished in a little beaded bag around his neck for the small coin that would get me on the bus. I could only guess what the money meant to him for that seven mile bus journey for me. I never was able to find him again to repay him.

So, I don't know why I expected that Dikola's friends would be anything other than protective of me. I suppose I had heard so many negative things from Toni, I was beginning to believe my professed unpopularity.

We reached the ancient call box safely. I was not looking forward to taking the call, as I knew how much I would be hurting my gentle, innocent Mike.

'Hello, Cheryl,' he stuttered over the line, 'it's me, Mike.' My heart ached hearing the tone of his voice, his emotions so naked and vulnerable. A part of me wanted to hop on the next flight out and kiss away all of his worries, but this kind of deception hurts all parties. Dikola would be shattered as the looser, me for having to make so large a sacrifice and Mike, appearing to have all that he wanted on the outside, but missing the essential core, the love that he deserved and needed.

'Yes, I know it's you,' I replied, suddenly tired.

'Cheryl, please talk to me, I'm out of my mind with worry about you. Please tell me that you are all right.'

'Yes, Mike, I'm fit and well, please believe me, I don't want you to worry.'

'Is it really true, do you really love this Dikola? I just can't believe it of you.'

'I'm so sorry, Mike. I never meant to hurt you. Yes, it's true, I love Dikola.'

'Are you coming home? I mean, can we at least talk about this? Please Cheryl, I'm on my knees here, give me one last chance. We can work it out. I love you Cheryl. I'll forgive you the time with Dikola, but please come home.' He was sobbing on the phone in great gasps. I couldn't give him anything but my apologies. I found myself crying with him, for his grief and for the promise of the life that we never seemed to manage to have together.

'Put Dikola on the phone,' he begged. Dikola nodded and I handed him the receiver.

'Please, please, I beg you as the husband of Cheryl, give me back my wife. Please.' The other warriors looked on, chatting amongst themselves. They could not understand why a grown man would be crying over a woman. Most of them had cows in their fields who had higher emotional value than any woman. They all thought that there must be something really special about me that a grown man would cry over my loss. I could hear Mike still on the line with Dikola, begging. We finally had to hang up on his grief. He was not to be consoled.

When Dikola got off the phone all of the warriors were looking on with big eyes. Dikola broke down in tears.

They began to chat in their native tongues in excited voices. I had certainly brought the place to life and given them stories for later. They loved stories. They called out to Dikola and he responded 'Yes, yes, but I love her more.' With that we were escorted back to our room.

It is the school holidays and Richelle and I are going to the children's matinee at the cinema. There is an old man sitting next to my sister. He whispers something to her and sends her off with a sixpence to get some ice cream. Richelle hisses to me to sit with the old man whilst she is away. I am frightened of her and do as she says.

The old man leans over me, whispering that I too can have a sixpence, but will have to reach into his pocket to get it. I reach into his trouser pocket and my hand grazes something warm and hard. The man grabs my hand and starts to rub it against the thing. The skin is loose and seems to move with my hand. Terrified, I try to grab my hand away. He holds tightly to my arm, forcing my hand down ever more firmly onto the warmth in his pocket. He is making horrible nasty noises, scaring me.

In the dim light of the cinema I search for my sister. Shouldn't she be back by now? I watch as she moves down the aisle to sit four rows ahead of me and the filthy man I am sitting with. I try desperately to scream to her, to anybody, for help. I can't seem to make a sound. I try again to lurch away, prayers racing through my head.

I feel a firm hand at the back of my head, the old man trying to force my face into his lap. Suddenly the darkness is cut by an usher's red torch.

'Get on out,' she growls, sticking her torch right into the man's jowly face, 'get out and don't let me catch you here again. I'll call the police on you, so I will.' She turns to me, her features softening.

'Are you all right my little darling? Has he hurt you? Are you here all alone?'

I tell her where my sister is and the usher goes over to speak with her. Richelle comes back, punching me in the stomach as the usher turns away.

Dikola had been really upset by the conversation with Mike. He got on his hands and knees and prayed to God to forgive him for all the pain that he was causing Mike. I broke down with him and we held each other, giving strength and comfort. Dikola was so upset that he had to run out to become violently ill.

We ended the night by drinking too much and crying ourselves to sleep. We would think about what to do tomorrow.

Chapter Eleven

Mike called the next day as I thought he might. He was very drunk and started out saying basically what he had gone over the night before. He became angry when he realised that I was not going to change my mind.

I was glad of his anger. I knew that if he could be angry with me he would start to heal. He called me horrible names and damned me to ghastly fates. I sat and took it. In a way I thought I deserved it, particularly when I thought of my children. Finally I coaxed him down and hung up the phone. I continued to hear from him once or twice a week, each time he was a little stronger, and finally he stopped being so angry.

Our life was becoming more and more difficult as the money grew short. I seemed to be giving money to so many other people's misfortunes that I was creating my own. Both Dikola and I had begun to drink, the alcohol numbing some of the more difficult realities of the situation.

I was finding it difficult to grow accustomed to all of the dirt and the almost complete lack of washing facilities. The shower was simply a tap over the open pit of the toilet. I refused to use this and instead would use an outside closet room that had a cold tap in the wall. I would throw the murky water over myself twice and sometimes three times a day.

I was so afraid of infection that I kept my mouth and nose covered with a bandana when I went to the toilet. I had run out of my anti-malaria medication and was terrified of any illness.

I was washing all of our clothing in cold water and a cheap washing powder that seemed to eat through our clothes very rapidly.

On one occasion Dikola borrowed an iron from someone. I was busy responding to one of Mike's letters and when I looked up at Dikola I saw him put the iron, still plugged into the socket, into a bowl of water. I was so shocked that I could not move to say anything or attempt to stop him. He took the iron from the water and began to happily iron his clothes. I found my voice and said, very slowly and carefully, 'Put the iron on the table and unplug it right now.' Noting the urgency in my voice he did as he was told and I told him of the danger that he had put himself in. God was watching.

Later in the day he rushed into the room because I was screaming at a cockroach that was scurrying across the floor. He laughed at my alarm, saying that with the way I was carrying on one would think I was being attacked by a mighty beast instead of just witnessing the wanderings of a bug. He picked it up for me and took it outside.

When he returned he was still laughing. He put his beaded blue and white bracelets around each of my ankles. He took off his warrior beads and put them around my neck, pulling me towards him.

'This means that you are my woman forever,' he said. He tightened them so they bit the skin, his eyes boring into me. 'I would love for you to be my wife for real one day. I love you so much. You make me crazy, woman, I love you forever. I want you to come home with me and meet my family. Come to Samburu with me and meet all of my people. I think that you have the guts for it.'

'Yes,' I agreed, 'I have the guts.'

We are woken up by the sound of Mum's shrieks of pain and the dull slapping of leather on flesh. Richelle and I creep quietly down the hall to see.

When we get to her Mum is whimpering like a puppy. Her back is lacerated with whip marks, as are her legs.

Her face is bloody and swollen with newly made bruises. Daddy grabs her by her hair despite, or maybe because of, our cries pleading with him to stop. He drags her in this fashion down the dimly lit corridor to the kitchen. I see him grab a pair of kitchen scissors and hold my breath.

Mummy goes very still, anticipating the downwards motion of the sharpened blades. My mind seems to be stuck in a constant loop of thought, taunting me with the knowledge that this is the end and I am, as ever, powerless.

He diverts the sharpened tool from its lethal course and proceeds to chop off all of her hair at the roots, inexpertly. Richelle and I flee to the bedroom, clinging to each other in a tangled heap, sobbing about the death we are certain was imminent.

'Our Father who art in heaven hallowed be thy name thy kingdom come thy will be done on earth as it is in heaven give us this day our daily bread and forgive us our trespasses as we forgive those who trespass against us and lead us not into temptation but deliver us from evil for thine is the kingdom and the power and the glory for ever and ever Amen,' Richelle and I breathe, hoping that our whispered prayers will act as a shield against the beast in the neighbouring room.

Moonlight is streaming into our bedroom through the window, onto the spot where we kneel on the hard linoleum. Richelle whispers that Jesus lives on the moon and that when he turns on all of the lights in his house the moon glows so brightly that we can see it from the earth.

'I'd like to see Jesus' house some day.' I whisper back.

'Someday you will.' soothes my sister. 'Someday we both will.'

'Do you think that's where Mummy is going tonight?'

'Maybe.'

'If Mummy goes I want to go too.'

'You and me both,' agrees Richelle.

Our thoughts are broken by the sound of the front door opening and Mum's renewed screams. We creep silently to the front door and peek out.

Dad has dumped Mum, naked, onto the cold stone of the fetid hallway and is biting her and hitting her. She fights back, supporting herself on the bannister of the stairwell. Her tenacity further fuels his anger and he grabs her under his arm, threatening to toss her out the window to the icy pavement, fifty feet below.

None of our neighbours will come to help, I know. He terrorises them as he does his own family, and is therefore feared. He gets the hallway window open and is just about to pass Mummy out head first when the pounding of footsteps is heard on the stairs, heralding the arrival of the police. Mummy is given a coat to cover herself and Dad is taken away.

Samburu is an arid land one thousand miles from Mombasa in northern Kenya. It is a vast open place with various tribes still existing by the same traditions they have observed for centuries. Anthropologists know it as the cradle of mankind.

We would be travelling as paupers, paying pittances for buses and any other means of four wheeled or legged transport we could find.

Our last attempt to go had been a bit of a disaster. Toni and Luria had arranged the car for the four of us, Brian having the sense to stay back at the hotel.

A man arrived for us in Mtwapa at the appointed time, driving a 1970's blue estate car for this one thousand mile trip. I took one look at it and burst out laughing. It couldn't possibly go a thousand feet, much less all the way to Samburu. The old clunker was held together with string, rust and a spot of Sellotape.

Besides us, the car contained a woman with two small children who were going to Nairobi, another Masai - Sammy, our luggage, bags of old clothes, six water barrels and an odd assortment of bit and pieces, including an anchor chain my feet were resting on. The tyres were completely bald.

As I took my place in the front seat, my dress tore from one end to the other. Dikola tried to find me another set of clothes, but could not seem to work out which bag was which. Toni was complaining bitterly, the other Masai were talking loudly in Maa, trying to speak over one another. Toni threw a box of photographs onto my lap, to get them out from under her feet.

The door on Toni's side was opened as an affluent looking black man with a leather brief case tried to catch a lift with us. Toni was climbing the walls by now.

'Luria,' she started, 'Luria tell me, tell me, where are you going to put him and his briefcase? Luria, read my lips, look at me when I am speaking, Luria, answer me.' Mule that Luria is, he never speaks when he doesn't want too and it wound Toni up. Briefcase Man got his walking orders.

We finally got all of our various bits tucked into almost bearable positions and the car pulled away from the curb, chugging away at fifteen miles per hour. At this rate it would take us five days to reach our destination. I prayed to God to make something happen so that we would not have to continue on this disaster of a trip.

Just then it started to pour. All of the windows of the car were open and Toni howled at me to roll up my window so that her photos would not get wet. I tried to do as she asked and the handle came off. The driver turned on the wipers and one lonely wiper came up slowly and then jerked to a stop, exhausted. The window on my side fell out. The car began to pack it in all together and slowed to five miles per hour. I went into a fit of giggles and soon the whole car was roaring with them.

We found a garage to pull into. The driver found that he could not open his door and had to crawl out of the window. Dikola followed him. I tried to open the door on my side, but that was also stuck fast.

The car started to roll back into the busy street we had just pulled off. I tried to stop it with the hand brake, but it was stuck. The laughter stopped as everyone in the car began to panic. I called to Dikola to help. He dived through the window and pulled up the hand brake with both hands just as the back wheels touched the road.

They got the car going again and two hours later we arrived back in Mtwapa, still laughing.

On this occasion, our second go, we were going to try and rely on public transport. We boarded a bus in Mombasa at eight in the evening which was to arrive in Nairobi at four the next morning.

Dikola, I found, was a very nervous traveller. He was chewing small sticks of something called *mirra*, a mild drug with caffeine-like effects. He was not one to take the drug in any quantity most of the time and I was surprised at the rate that he was consuming the stuff. He explained that he wanted to stay awake so that we would not be robbed or assaulted. Though he was not a great fan of the stuff, many of his people were, almost living on that and snuff.

We stopped off in a shanty town, where there was a man selling knives. Dikola took this opportunity to buy a very intimidating looking weapon, saying he was taking no chances with me.

Chapter Twelve

Dikola told me to go ahead and get some sleep once we were back on the coach, promising he would keep an eye on me. He kept on kissing me in the dim light of the coach and held to my hand tightly. Eventually I did sleep, waking in Nairobi at five in the morning. It would not be light until six thirty and we would not be allowed off until this time as it was felt to be too dangerous.

The next part of the journey would be by van. This would go another two hundred miles and would cost a further £1.50. I was pinned tightly against the window of the van, which was loaded to a dangerous level. The sweat flowed like water and the constant shaking of the bus put me into a trance-like state.

Finally we reached the end of the van's route, a dusty little town full of wooden kiosks nailed together crudely. There seemed to be a huge junk yard off to the side filled with old clothing, mostly cheap imports. We waited here for three hours until the next bus was full enough to justify its leaving.

This part of the trip was on a straight road and you could see for miles in any direction. Dead zebras lay in the road where they had been hit, but we could see live members of the herd galloping across the dusty plains. The scenery was breath-taking. The rift valley looked like a giant hole gaping to the centre of the earth. We passed one sign announcing that we had reached the equator, and then another sign which claimed the same thing.

Again we changed vehicles to a different truck that would take us a further one hundred miles. Dikola had told me previously that he made this trip once a month to bring supplies to his family; fifteen siblings, his parents and his father's other wife. I was now starting to fully appreciate what Dikola had to go through as the family's only bread winner and my own problems seemed insignificant.

In the next town we stopped at we bought some tea, sugar, rice and sweets for the smaller children. It would have been unacceptable to go home without these provisions, as no outsider would ever consider entering another's house without bearing gifts.

I found I was becoming impatient with Dikola. I would yell at him and he would try to drag me away from the group so that I could scream in private and embarrass him less. I was becoming short tempered with his lack of knowledge of western culture and my own lack of understanding about his. We were trying so hard to fathom each other but were finding that we had stumbling blocks that at times seemed insurmountable. We knew our only glue was our love for each other. We had no cultural common ground, we were trying to build a life on feelings alone. We were both tired from the trip and I was afraid that if things continued as they were we would have very little left to say to each other once we were there.

The next truck proved to be our last. We drove along for only an hour before the track ended and we had to get out to walk the rest of the way, about twenty minutes.

I stopped on a rise to look at the land. I couldn't see any sign of human habitation; it felt like we were alone at the edge of the world. I squeezed Dikola's hand for reassurance.

'Cheryl,' he warned, 'my parents and people are very primitive.'

'I know,' I said, suddenly nervous 'it's all right. That's just life.'

We made our way up a hill of cracked, dry mud. When we reached the top we were facing a small square enclosure with a wooden base covered with a mixture of cow dung and mud. The roof was of a similar stuff and the entire structure was a mere six feet tall. The building was almost indistinguishable from the rest of the thirsty landscape.

Suddenly people appeared as if from nowhere calling out greetings I didn't understand but knew to be friendly. I nodded politely and hoped I was not causing offence.

The *kaaji*, mud house, had a double entrance in a sort of 'n' to keep out the lions and other beasts which might consider sniffing a little too close. Inside reeked of smoke and dead animals. The oily scent clung to everything it touched and in all the time I spent in Samburu I was never quite free of it. It was very dark as the only light came from the perpetual fire crackling in the hearth and some small cracks in the walls.

We sat in a small group to one side of the enclosure with Dikola's family. I watched them in conversation, straining to pick up the few words that I was familiar with.

His mother seemed a very meek and gentle woman and his father a powerful elder. Dikola was popular amongst his people, well liked and also respected. I loved him all the more seeing these rough beginnings and how he still persevered and was treasured amongst his own people.

This was to be my home for the time I was in Samburu. The conditions were extremely rough, as few concessions had been made to western technology. Dikola never left my side for a second, knowing the dangers of the bush and my ignorance of all of the potential hazards. He even followed me out when I had to use the loo, as I had visions of being bit in the bum by some poisonous snake and dying with my kanga up above my knees.

Dikola's people were very good to me, boiling water for my baths and giving me all the privacy my modesty required. Dikola and I were given our own hut to sleep in at night. We lay on raised mud platforms covered with cow hides, surrounded by giant spears. A luxury, as most Masai sleep their entire families in the one room huts. Had I not been there Dikola would have slept in his mother's house on a similar raised pallet reserved for the warriors in the family.

The fire burned all day and night in these huts, stinging my eyes and lungs. The night is cold in Samburu, as there is rarely a cloud cover to keep the warmth, and the fire aids in keeping away any wild animals that may make it through the oddly shaped entrance. There were no blankets, so Dikola kept me warm at night.

I am sitting at a table in the nursery, waiting for one of the helpers to bring me my lunch. The helper is approaching and she looks like she is swaying. Forward and back. I am in a wooden chair, sandy coloured with a high back. My mind keeps on telling me to switch off. Just switch off. Now. I do.

The chair is digging into my back, hurting like hell. I can't do anything about it. I simply can't move an inch. I tried, but my body won't respond.

I feel myself lifted out of the chair by a man and lowered into a children's camp bad. Everyone is poking me, tickling me, lifting my clothes off. I can hear them and feel them, but can't respond. Inside I am screaming.

I recall one morning during which the sun woke us through a slit in the wall, earlier than Dikola was ready to rise. He grabbed a clean new towel out of my bag and jammed it into the hole. I was amused by the action because the towel meant as little to him as a rag might. He did not see it as something old or new but rather as something with a clear purpose, valuable for this reason only.

Dikola is an amazing person, living his life straddling both worlds in an attempt to make sense of either. I saw his native life as an existence mirroring the primordial past, waiting in stasis for western man to burn himself out and return to roots long forgotten. It seemed like God had kept back a handful of his children to wait until the end of the world to begin to live again the way he originally intended, one with nature and autonomous within their own circles. The keepers of the faith.

I woke up early in this place always, and would sit on the cow hide bed I shared with Dikola, wearing a kanga and little else, often waking him with a kiss. Making love in the bush of Africa stripped away all inhibitions, made it the most basic and essential of all functions for the moments that it lasted. I would forget myself, reaching only for the sexual power that can be found in the Eve of all woman. I discovered in myself a sensual, sexual being who had enough need to kill off any man. I would wake him with my mouth, sometimes rolling off of the cowhide into the hearth in the middle of the hut, burning ourselves and not noticing. I never worried that I would become pregnant, despite our lack of precautions, I knew that I would be fine.

I had asked God to not allow me to be pregnant and we would make love for hours on the floor of Dikola's hut. We would often stop in fits of giggles, as I would be as black as he from the mud and charcoal on the floor. It was the sexiest thing on earth and all modern variations suddenly seemed a dangerous insult to nature.

The life of these people is extremely difficult. I ate very little during my time there, losing two stone from my rather portly figure. The diet consisted primarily of rice made oily with chicken bones and a sweet black tea, as well as water drawn either from a well or a neighbour's rain bucket.

After a few days Dikola and I walked into the village of Maralal, an eighteen kilometres walk across lion country. When we arrived I bought a lemonade and opened it, thinking that I would never again enjoy something as much as I would this drink.

As I raised the bottle to my lips a small boy materialised at my side, his clothes torn and his dirty little penis bared for all to see. I gave the drink to him, which he finished quickly, running back to the shop to renew the bottle for a few shillings.

Chapter Thirteen

The sun sets quickly in Kenya, and by the time Dikola and I had gone only half of the eighteen kilometres home the veil of darkness had fallen. Dikola could see in this darkness, though I was nearly blind to anything not within a few yards of me. When we were about half an hour from the house, Dikola stopped sharply, causing me to fall against him. He explained that ahead he could smell and see a herd of elephants. We hid under a bush, our eyes straining to see the herd. My eyes were becoming accustomed to the dark and within one hundred yards of where we hid I could see the dim shapes of the pachyderm.

As I caught my breath at the size of the magnificent beasts, Dikola loosened the knot of the sheet he was wearing as a kanga and draped it over me. He then squatted in front of me, burying himself under the sheet with me. In this way we came to resemble an animal and were able to walk amongst the elephants without them taking note of us.

I knew I should be afraid of the animals we were walking amidst, but somehow with Dikola I could find no reason to be afraid.

When we were a safe distance from the giant beasts Dikola removed his white cloth from my back and wrapped it tightly around his body like a shroud. He stood on a mound before me, staring at the endless blanket of stars above us. The moon had risen and it shone upon him, making the white of his sheet seem to glow. His eyes moved to me silently.

He then shot his gaze into the sky, throwing his arms up into the air as if to follow it. The kanga billowed around him like the wings of a swan. He said something to the sky in his language in a high, keening voice that caused shivers to run up my spine. He beckoned to me and I stood by his side as he draped the blanket around me and lifted my arm so that we looked like a double butterfly.

'Look,' he said, 'look, we are angels, we are angels of the night.' I began to quiver. Dikola burst away from my side into the moonlit valley with the kanga trailing behind him, singing a melancholy song in his high sweet voice. He returned to where I stood and kissed the moisture from my cheeks. I realised I had been crying.

He wrapped the billowing fabric around me and we fell to the floor of the valley making love under the watchful eye of God.

There was one Masai, Million, who suited his name quite well, as he was quite wealthy amongst his people, having a three room house made of wood and concrete, built for him by a friend from Switzerland. He also had the luxuries of a rain barrel and a shower enclosure, both of which he was very generous with. I would shower under the stars in the icy water with only a curtain between me and the rest of the world thinking this was indeed heaven.

One night whilst performing this ritual, I happened to peer out of the curtain of the enclosure. I spotted a lioness about one hundred yards away from me trying to break into the cattle enclosure. Apparently the warriors spotted the menace about the same time that I did as they let out a mighty cry and came running with their giant spears.

The lioness was just as disconcerted by all of the noise as I was, because she darted away only a few yards past where I was bathing. I felt no fear.

The Samburu boys thought me terribly brave, as they assumed most white people would have screamed at the sight of a lioness such as this one coming so close. They had previously heard the story of the elephants and also of the roach from Dikola and thought it was terribly funny that I would be frightened by something as small as a bug, but be brave about an elephant and a lioness.

It was during this time they gave me the Samburu name of Nicmarie. I was so flattered, particularly since I am told I am the only white woman to be given a tribal name. Dikola was very proud.

I brought some of the children's outgrown clothes with me to be distributed amongst Dikola's siblings. I had a very pretty pink dress of Chloie's which I slipped over the head of Dikola's four year old sister. She cried and danced around the mud hut, disbelieving her great good fortune. I don't believe I will ever forget that day. I think of all the joy the soft cotton of the frilly dress caused her and how easy it has become for children of our culture to take such things for granted. I knew then how important it was for me to help these people who had been so good to me. My heart may never be the same again.

The life in Samburu was beginning to take its toll on me. My health was now suffering, most likely from the microbes in the well water which I had been foolish enough to drink. I knew if I was to regain my health and ultimately, to survive, I would have to get home. I had spent all my money on food and medical supplies for the people around me and was now in a quandary as to where to get the money for my ticket home. When Dikola's people realised just how sick I had become they tried to scrape up every shilling amongst them to make up the money for the flight, knowing I would send the money back to them as soon as I possibly could.

I was able to call Mike and he was kind enough to agree to send me the money I had waiting on loan from the bank to the British embassy back in Nairobi. I would have to get the money and go to Gulf Air and hope they would have a deal good enough for me to afford.

I was missing my children and was desperate to get home for my son Tommie's birthday on the ninth of May.

I was getting so sick that finally I had to stay on the cow hide in the hut and take a foul tasting medicine Dikola's mother had prepared for me. It was made of some sort of tree bark and roots with a bit of honey to cut some of the bitterness. Dikola fed me spoonful by spoonful until I got a little stronger.

We were finally able to leave Samburu on the eighth of May. I was still too ill to travel and distraught that I was to miss my son's birthday. I had promised him repeatedly that I would make every effort to be there for his birthday and felt truly evil for having to break such a crucial promise. I had put my own selfish needs before those of my children and knew myself to be failing miserably in my chosen role as mother. I had no idea I could be so hard.

I had come to realise that part of the reason for my going to Kenya and being with Dikola was to recover from my mangled childhood. It had helped me to recover my patience and my sanity. I was learning more about myself here than I ever thought possible.

The people from social services are sending me to see a psychologist to see if they can figure out why I have been having so many physical problems in school; vomiting, blackouts, hysterical paralysis.

A part of me understands the nature of these sessions and covers for me, hiding the sins of my family. I don't know if it is simply my mother's suggestion that causes my actions or if they are related to one of the different personalities that seem to affect me at times of profound stress.

One night I am woken up by noises coming from the front room. I recognise my father's voice, but not the feminine one and go to investigate. Through the gap in the door I can see an unfamiliar woman with large breasts moving to some internal music, plying the soft area between her legs with phallic objects and moaning. Just to the side of the bed stands my father, recording the strange woman's actions on film.

I slip quietly from my the door and out the front door to the communal toilet. I lock myself in and become violently ill.

The next time I visit the psychiatrist I want desperately to share with her the events of that night. Instead I begin to dig into the cool sand of the box kept in the children's area. I find a doll and bury her in the fine grains.

'Is there something wrong, Cheryl?' the lady asks. I point to the spot where the doll is buried.

'There,' I say, 'Suzanne is there and she is dead forever.'

'Why Cheryl, why is the doll dead? Why is Suzanne dead?'

'She will not move,' I answer.

'Isn't Suzanne your middle name? You are here, alive and well in front of me.'

'She is dead, dead, dead,dead, dead, I put her in the sand. Leave her there, I will come and see her next time and then you too can see that she is dead.'

'O.K., Cheryl, we can do that.'

We said our goodbyes to Dikola's tribe. The parting seemed very unemotional, though a few of the younger ones ran off crying. His mother kissed both of my cheeks and embraced me as she thought was my custom. I accepted her farewell with a heavy heart as I did not know when I would see her again, or if I would ever make her simple dreams come true.

Chapter Fourteen

Dikola and I had to walk again to Maralal to find a truck to take us part of the way back to Nairobi. I made it, but was feeling very weak by the time we arrived. When we boarded the bus my period started, unscheduled. I was bleeding in copious amounts and began to suspect that I might actually be miscarrying. I had to tear up a kanga to staunch the bleeding. The blood was running down my legs and I felt I might pass out.

The next bus hadn't any seats and we had to stand for hours during the long delay. When we did start out the tyre burst and I thanked God for sending us a sober driver who was able to keep the bus from overturning.

At the next stop I went in to use the bathroom and found a dirty bandage which, in my anaemic stupor, I made into a tampon. I had to take off all of my clothes and throw them away, as they were too soaked in blood to ever be worn again. I had to wear a couple of kangas after this and I smelled awful, something that worried me more than being sick.

We were almost completely broke by the time we got to Nairobi and had to check into a very seedy hotel that cost the equivalent of three pounds. An English prison seemed luxurious next to the cess pit that we were in. The toilet room was covered in diarrhoea. I was sure that I had died in that bus after all and gone to hell. We both prayed to God as we were very anxious about our surroundings and felt exceedingly unsafe.

Dikola washed me down in cold water as my fever had become so high and I rested as much as I could. The proprietor came to our door at two-thirty in the morning and Dikola opened the door dressed in full warrior gear. He had arrived dressed in his ill fitting western clothes and the man had not previously realised that he was a Masai, member of the most feared of all African tribes. He had his rungu hidden behind his back in case of trouble.

'What do you want here at this time of night, disturbing my wife and I?' Dikola asked defiantly. He brought out the rungu from its hiding pace. The man flustered quickly and made his excuses, padding quickly back down the hall.

I can't find my sister to walk to playschool with this afternoon. As I begin to trudge in the direction of the school by myself, I suddenly have an overpowering urge to go home. I start to walk in that direction, faster and faster into a run. I race along the streets until I feel my lungs will burst. My shoe falls off, so I pick it up and remove the other, running barefoot down the filthy streets. I pick up a piece of glass in my foot, but ignore it. Ever faster I run, until I arrive at the front door, groping for the key hanging by a ribbon around my neck.

I find the key, lose it and find it again, letting myself into the flat. My breath catches in my throat, listening. I can hear Humperdink's 'Please Release Me' playing down the hallway, in Mum's and Dad's room. Mum usually leaves music playing, to fool any intruders into thinking that there is somebody in the house. I am anxious about being home, as I am supposed to be in play school. After what seems like an eternity the record ends and restarts. I let out my breath. Nobody is home. I go back to the bedroom to switch off the gramophone.

As I venture down the hallway, the record sticks, repeating 'release me, release me.' When I arrive in the bedroom I find Mum standing in the window sill above the tracks, checking her watch. 'The train is coming, the train is coming, the train is coming,' says a voice in my head. 'Don't scream,' I think.

The glass in my foot begins to sting and I look down, remembering it. I have left a trail of small brown stains in my wake, and I can see a mark forming on the carpet, oozing past my toes.

I approach my mother's restless form slowly, composing my features into an expression of pain. I touch my mum gently, just tapping her with my fingers. As she looks down at me, I pick up my foot, gesturing to the small shard embedded in it.

'I cut my foot, Mum. I got glass in it so the teacher sent me home,' I lie.

The train passes under us and Mum sighs, crawling from the window. She leans wearily on my shoulder, heavy in her skinny frame.

'Let's fix you,' she says, and goes to fetch some water.

Dikola decided at this time that our lives were in great danger and that we were in a nest of thieves and crooks. He said that they were probably planning to rob or even murder us to take the little that we still carried. In the room where they had put us was a second door leading to the room to our immediate right. They would have easy access if they wanted it.

The following morning we told them that we would be staying longer than expected and would plan on bringing the money that evening. We planned instead to make our escape that afternoon.

As we were leaving the British embassy with the money Mike had transferred that morning we bumped into a relative of Dikola's. He asked us where we were staying and the young man stiffened at our response. After the initial response he started speaking with Dikola in rapid Swahili saying he was shocked we were still alive, and must plan how to get our things away from the place safely.

We planned that we would get a taxi to the outside of the hotel, where I would wait for them to come out with the cases. We started down the street to look for a suitable taxi, being one that was not white, as they were meant for tourists and charged double the normal rates.

I walked through downtown Nairobi with Dikola on one side and his relative, Paul, on the other. I was wearing a large green skirt and had Dikola's rungu hidden in the folds. Dikola was carrying all of my essential documents and money in the inside pocket of his jacket. I was still unwell and remained quiet while Paul and Dikola busily made plans about our things and where we were to stay for the next few days.

Suddenly I was surrounded by three black men. They were sticking their hands in my pockets and down my top and were frisking my sides. Dikola reached towards me with his left hand and my hand that was stabilising the rungu shot out. He quickly grabbed the weapon and I shot my arms into the air, leaving the men free access to frisk me, throwing them off guard.

Dikola attacked the three of them at once. He let out a high wailing noise which caused the thieves to run away shouting that Dikola was a Masai and they must run quickly. Dikola was very disconcerted by the encounter and shook for the rest of the day. By now I was too ill to worry about anything as trivial as potential death.

We found our taxi and put our plan into action, rescuing our cases from the creepy hotel. Dikola's relative kindly offered us a place to stay just outside of the Nairobi airport where some of the family members worked. They were generous enough to give us a bed for the two nights that I would be waiting for the plane and treated us well. I repaid their kindness the best I could.

The family did all of their cooking on a stove that was dangerously low. On the second day that I was there the daughter of the family was left to play alone in the kitchen area and fell against the stove where some water was boiling. She fell against the stove and must have caught the underside of her arm on some of the hot metal of it. The child began screaming *'Moto, moto, moto!'* (Hot, hot, hot!) and the mother seemed not to know what to do with the child and seemed to be unclear even about what had happened to her.

I picked up the child, ill though I was, and ran with her to the outside loo, where I knew there to be a bucket of cool water. I put my hands in the cold water and flicked it on her face, as she had gone very still and I feared that she may have gone into shock. This seemed to revive her some and I began to throw cold water over the angry red burn. She revived a little and began to cry, of which I was glad.

I brought her back to the house with the water and found a handkerchief and kept on wetting in the water, wrapping it around the wound to make a cold compress. The mother then recognised what I was doing was comforting the child and took over, saying 'Asante sana' (Thank you very much). I went to the shop and bought her some children's pain killer, giving her a dose and hoping she would sleep. She fell asleep within an hour and was fine the next day, except for a large blister on her arm.

The night before departure we had the whole house to ourselves. We made love despite me being so ill, and neither of us could stop crying at the thought of our imminent separation. We couldn't sleep that night and instead brought in the dawn, watching the morning star rise over Nairobi.

I felt a tangible sadness inside me. The tears rolled around in my brain, unshed. We found a bus to hire to take us to the airport, as there were no taxis to be hired in this part of Nairobi.

The whole family came to see me off at the airport, but I only really wanted Dikola and it made the farewell that much more painful. I gave twenty pounds to the family as a gesture of goodwill and eighty pounds to Dikola, as it was all he would have to tide him over until the next tourist season. He had already missed all of the proceeds from the last two; he had not worked because of me.

I left for the departure lounge at the last possible moment, not wanting the moment to arrive too soon. Dikola and I clung to each other in mute disbelief. The moment we both dreaded but deemed necessary had arrived. I was violently aware of how filthy I was, having not been able to bath properly since we had left Samburu. I wanted to be able to cry, to have some kind of a release, but somehow the tears would not come.

Dikola clasped me tightly, kissing me and burying his face in my hair, sobbing out the words 'I love you, I love you, goodbye Cherie Nicmarie. Come back to me,' over and over. I finally could take no more and headed for passport control, determined not to look back over my shoulder at Dikola. I couldn't help myself, and stopped shortly before the barrier that would have separated him from me physically.

I spun around and saw him walking slowly backwards, the tears running unchecked down his cheeks.

Before I got to the plane I had to rush to the toilet. My stool had been loose for the past month and this combined with the minimal amount of substantial food available to me had caused me to lose two stones in only a short period of time. I stayed in the loo for an hour, trying to pull myself together enough to get onto the plane.

I boarded the plane just in time and sat down next to a woman who was on her way to Southampton. I was very conscious of my smell at this point and was still menstruating heavily. I spent some of the time in the bathroom cleaning up as best I could, though the woman was kind enough not to say anything.

I was falling in and out of sleep. My seat-mate woke me repeatedly, concerned as I kept on calling out Dikola's name in my sleep and crying. When I slept I felt that I could almost see him there with me. I thought of all of the things about him which made me laugh and cry.

I remembered our trip to the British Embassy. Dikola did not understand about metal detectors and how they would sense there was a knife on him. I urged him to give the guard his knife and he couldn't understand why I would coax him to do such a thing.

We took an elevator after that and I didn't know until it was in motion that Dikola had never been in one. I felt terrible for forgetting such simple things about where he had come from and who he was. How could I have expected him to know such things?

Chapter Fifteen

On one occasion whilst still in Mtwapa a mother brought me a child to cure who was burnt so badly it could never be properly cared for, certainly not in the existing conditions. They felt that because I was white I must know the magic of the doctors who had come to see them previously. They couldn't possible understand that all I had was a basic first aid certificate and the prayers I sent to God with each new healing.

I remembered a healing I performed on little Moses, one of the small relatives of Dikola's in Mombasa. He had cut his foot to bits on a tin can. They waited for two days until I was next scheduled to visit them because they trusted no one else. He was not yet two years old with the fragile immune system of a child and the infection had already been left to fester for two days. I got some spring water and tossed four water detoxifying tablets into it, some T.C.P. and some Dettol and had his parents hold him tight whilst I forced his foot into the burning liquid. He needed stitches really, the wound was so deep and he screamed loudly, protesting the pain. All of the dead skin came off in the mixture, however, and I was able to wrap the clean skin in a fresh bandage.

I cleaned his little foot in the same manner for two days in a row, praying hard each time. Within three days his foot was well on the road to recovery and he was running around barefoot with his friends again.

His sister had come to me previously with an enormous, painful abscess on her back. I put a compress of magsolphate paste on it overnight and two days later she was fine, running about and playing with all of the rest of the children. I felt so useful and worthwhile during my time in Kenya.

I am sitting in the kitchen eating my Cornflakes whilst Mum and Dad's live-in girlfriend, Doreen, stand at the work top talking. I looked at my food and then to my mother and back again.

Suddenly I drop my spoon into my bowl, gaining the attention of all in the room.

I get up and walk to my mother on my knees, grabbing fast to her legs. I gaze at her face and beg her in my strongest voice to leave my father. I tell her that if she doesn't leave him, he will kill us all.

Doreen followed suit, grabbing my mother's arm, telling her that she must leave and leave now, if not for her sake, then for the children.

These are the memories that haunted me on the trip home whilst the stewardess' brought me water to sip to reduce the fever that was causing my vivid recollections.

It seemed on the plane that I was still in one of the cramped mud huts. I felt as if the walls were coming in at me and then receding, coming in and going again. I could see the lion's bright eyes boring into me and could feel the cockroaches and snakes falling from their rafter homes onto my naked body. I could see the burnt and mutilated bodies of small children lying about and others falling down holes, begging for my assistance. I felt myself falling into the mouth of a child who had grown large enough to swallow me. I was buried alive and the maggots were eating my still viable flesh.

I screamed in my sleep and the kindly woman next to me roused and comforted me once again. The remainder of the trip to my connecting flight in Abu Dabi was a similar sequence of nightmares and memories.

The airport was amazing. It seemed so clean after what I had been living through for the past few months and the past few hours in my mind. I went into the toilets, so clean you could eat off of the floor and washed completely, taking off most of my clothes as I could no longer summon the will to care about modesty. I still felt so ill.

I finally left the toilets and sat in one of the plush lounges, waiting for my connecting flight. A doctor approached me, saying he had been watching me on the flight and was very worried about me. He told me he was a member of the Christian Society in Nairobi, and something in my heart told me to trust him. I took the malaria pills he offered me. I felt so horribly weak and sick and ended up falling asleep on a sofa in the lounge. I woke up in time for my second flight.

I arrived in England after twenty hours of travelling on the fourteenth of May, the day before my thirty-fourth birthday. I still had three hours to travel before arriving at the Isle of Wight.

I came to my door at two in the afternoon and found that I didn't have my key and had to leave my bags with a neighbour. Having done this I went immediately to the doctor. They saw me straight away and sent me to the hospital. I was put into a private ward and subjected to blood test after blood test to determine the source of my ailment. They seemed to be having trouble getting the blood at all, with one doctor putting a needle through a nerve. I was in no mood for all of this as I was already so drained emotionally and physically. I felt myself becoming angry and abusive and begged them to just leave me alone.

Mike came in a bit later with the children and started in on me immediately. The children looked so very sad and I felt horrible realising what I had put them through since the previous summer. Mike, with his usual tact, suggested that I looked so ill, maybe I had AIDS. He had never seen me so slim before. Did I have any idea what Dikola had been up to in the past?

I was so taken aback by his venom I reacted too slowly. Stevie ran from the room crying before I had a chance to say anything. Tommie looked resentfully at Mike. Chloie just seemed happy to be with her mother again.

I was tired and frustrated and feeling very much at odds with my surroundings saying, against my better instincts, 'Fuck off. Yes, that's right, I'm going to die from AIDS, then you'll be happy, won't you Mike?' I could think of nothing but what a cold unfeeling man he was, and how dare he be surprised when I chose to run off with someone else. After more of a debate the hospital sent Mike away, explaining I was far too sick to have visitors of this sort and to only come back when he was without the children. From this point no one was allowed into my room unless they were fully gowned, out of fear of infectious disease pending results from the lab.

Toni turned up the next night at a quarter past ten. She claimed to be there to cheer me up, saying chirpy things like 'well, you don't look sick to me'. I remember thinking 'Oh well, in that case let me go ahead and get knocked down by a lorry and maybe you will find that to be satisfactory.'

I told her of Mike's catty comment about AIDS and Toni agreed with him. This certainly seemed a possibility. 'What a sick bunch of people' I thought.

She continued, 'I am not a bit surprised you're ill after the way Dikola treated you. I mean you have not had sex for so long.

'This is all so sick,' I thought. 'What is she going on about? Maybe she was talking about the way she had been treated and didn't know how to say it.'

After eight days I was allowed to go home, after much pleading with the doctor. He was not very happy with letting me go as I was still terribly ill and he had yet to make a diagnosis. They allowed me to go on the condition of one month of bed rest and regular check-ups.

Chapter Sixteen

Back at home I was little short of mad. I felt like a crazy woman. I repeatedly experienced violent outbursts, screaming the most foul forms of abuse to anybody who dared to come near. I spat and swore, refused all food, alternately declined to speak and then showered abuse. I cried to the point of hysteria.

I was still losing a lot of weight, falling down to seven stones, ten pounds at the end of it all. I didn't like myself thin, it changed my whole personality. My hair was falling out in great bunches and my dementia was worsening. I insisted, despite the negative test results, that I was really ill. I just knew it.

Mike was incredibly patient during this time and would restrain and comfort me like one would a child. All the time I was calling for Dikola, begging him to go and find Dikola for me. I would apologise over and over again, asking him to forgive me for needing this man so much and feeling I could simply not go on without him. I was pathetic.

I went for days without washing or eating, just crying. I had nightmares and would scream out in the night, scaring the children. I had a recurring dream about a woman eating the limbs of small children with blood running down her face. I wouldn't allow the children into the room to see me during this time, knowing how traumatic it would be for them if they knew just how badly off I was. I was so ashamed of myself. Mike said he was sure I was going to die of a broken heart. He said he had read about it in a medical textbook and thought I suited the profile perfectly. He felt sad that now all he could do was try to make me as comfortable as possible whilst he watched my decline. My hair was falling out in large fist-fulls. Still the doctors found nothing.

Mike would sit with me day and night, rocking me like a child for comfort. He was my hope, my comfort. He promised he would do everything in his power to get me back to Dikola and Kenya. I knew my life depended on it, as did the children. I remember them crying so hard.

It was hell on earth and I found it impossible to do anything for them. I couldn't even be there. I was ill and grief stricken and none of this was their fault, yet they were the ones to suffer most profoundly for it. I thank God for giving me children who are so very strong.

I had a regular time once a week during which I was supposed to be able to get through on the telephone to Kenya and Dikola. On one occasion there was a problem and he wasn't able to make the connection on his end. I was hysterical, sure that death was the only thing that would keep him from the phone. Mike thought I was going to kill him and Chloie hid under the table. Tommie ran out of the house to get the police, so afraid was he of my rabid rage. I felt the part of me which was my father rise up in me and I threw the furniture and broke the glasses, thinking briefly of how Mike and I used to argue over them. I was shaking from head to foot and punching the walls and the work-tops.

Then I saw Chloie hunched under the table, terrified of her mother. Her fantastic blue eyes were red rimmed from crying. She crawled out hesitantly when I coaxed her and crawled into my arms, begging to know if the monster I had become had departed. We were sitting like this when Tommie came in with the police. We talked it out and all was fine.

Mummy wakes us up early this morning.

'Are we leaving Daddy?' I ask.

'Shut up Cheryl, get ready as quickly as you can.'

Richelle and I jump up, sensing Mum's urgency. Mum begins to busily gather up our clothes, asking us to gather up some favourite toys and to not ask any questions. I look tearfully at my splendid Wendy house, turn and leave.

We rush down the cold grey steps of the building, looking over our shoulders as we run, expecting him to be there at our heels.

'Jump into the taxi,' coaxes my mother, 'keep your heads down and don't come up until I tell you to.' We obediently crawl onto the floor. Mum stays up, gazing back, watching for any car that looks like Dad's; waiting for him to follow.

From our position on the floor, Richelle and I speculate and make up stories about living with Mum in a new place and how things are going to be so much better and different. We feel betrayed as the truth of our situation becomes apparent.

We take the train to Plymouth in Devon and have a taxi drop us in front of a large, industrial looking building. I hate it straight away. Tugging at my Mum's sleeve, I ask if we can go. There is no reply. I wander a bit, waiting for my mother to finish speaking with the adults. Dozens of children are about, looking at us with frank curiosity. I ignore them.

A woman approaches me, squatting on her heels so that we would be the same height.

'Your Mummy is going now.'

I spin away from the lady, grabbing for my mother.

'No, please Mummy, I want to come with you, why can't I come?' I plead, tears streaming down my face. She turns her heel and walks away. I cry after her, not understanding, despite the kindly adult voices around me. I try to flee, to catch her before she is gone, but I am restrained by two adults, who hold me fast.

I took to my bed again, still awaiting the hospital results. I was very bored and began to write letters to everyone I knew, not just Dikola. Mike was bringing me several different newspapers every day to keep me busy and I started to write to their agony columns. I would always leave these in the bin by the bed.

Mike came in periodically to see me and offer to make me food or get me anything at all. On one of these occasions he brought me the Wednesday edition of *The Sun* containing the women's supplement. There was a story in the middle about a white teacher who gave up everything for the love of a Gambian man half her age. She had enough money to start a business with him, however, and seemed to be in better straights than I was. I remember thinking my story was much better than that, but it had all been done, and mine certainly couldn't be of any interest to anyone.

Out of sheer boredom I went ahead and wrote a letter to the problem page and put it into the bin again. Mike came in to check on me again. He saw the letter I had just crumpled into the bin and offered to post it for me. I let him do it grudgingly, figuring I had nothing to lose.

I didn't think about the letter again, assuming nothing could possibly come of it. I carried on in my nasty temper, selfish as hell. Finally a letter came from the hospital requesting to see me. They discovered I had a rare infection which I had probably picked up from drinking the Samburu well water and using infected sanitary wear. I had to go back into the hospital for treatment and have a lumbar puncture to ensure the infection had not reached the nervous system. I was given several deep muscle injections.

I was told there was a distinct possibility Dikola could be ill also and if he was it would be necessary for him to return to England for treatment or he would die. I was horrified at this and it made me realise all the more what he meant to me. Mike was wonderful, saying he would sell the house to bring Dikola back if necessary.

I kept on dreaming that God was instructing me to sell my gold. He told me to go to a shop and sell my gold for the one hundred and five pounds the man would offer me and never look back. I took no notice, but the message was getting stronger. I pondered it for a few days and finally collected my little bit of gold and took it to the local jewellery shop. The salesman offered me one hundred and five pounds which I took readily, much to the man's surprise. The hairs on the back of my neck were standing on end, but I forced myself not to look back. What is gone is gone.

Life went on in the same manner, the only difference being I had added another drop of cash to the ocean of money that I needed for my next trip to Kenya.

Four days after the sale of the gold I got a call from *The Sun* newspaper. I was a little taken aback as I had forgotten all about the letter I had written almost three weeks before. The woman on the line explained that *The Sun* was willing to pay me one hundred pounds for a low key story in the Sun Women Section the following week. I said I would prefer to get back to her as I would have to discuss it with my family before I could make a decision. Mike and the children agreed to this and I was able to get a hold of Dikola also to gain his approval.

I was pleased that something so simple I had done had attracted so much attention and I would be paid for it. Laura, my contact with *The Sun*, explained that there was no rush as the article would not be run for a few weeks, but she would be sending around a photographer in the meantime.

The photographer came by in the beginning of Cowes Week. He had not called ahead and caught me unawares with no make-up early in the morning. I was alone in the house and he asked if he could start by taking a quick look around the house, to which I readily agreed, figuring I might take the opportunity to neaten myself up a bit. Much to my chagrin he followed me up to my bedroom, where he saw the picture of Dikola and I dressed in warrior gear.

He loved the picture and asked if I would be willing to dress as I was in the picture to make his photos more interesting. I couldn't see why not, so I went ahead and did it, doing a bit of a rush job of it, my make-up not quite right.

I looked tired and drawn, seeming to go through all of the motions like a poorly led marionette. I smiled as I was told and was serious as directed. Mike came home with the children and they got to join in the fuss. They were a bit fed up after the umpteenth photo and the photographer took his last pictures with the family looking as fed up as they had become. These are the ones which were printed.

The next day Laura Collins from the paper arrived to do the interview. She was a lovely person who bore a striking resemblance to Twiggy and was, at the time, six months pregnant. We got on very well from the start as she is a very easy going person.

She took me to a restaurant where we could talk. It was a Friday and her mobile phone kept on ringing, interrupting us. Eventually we got it done.

Chapter Seventeen

All weekend I was getting phone calls to help verify parts of the story. They called to say that they would be putting the story into the main part of the paper. A few hours later it was to be on two pages. Late Sunday it was to be on the front page of the Monday paper. I was shocked and just stood there, frozen on the spot.

They offered to pay for another trip to Kenya for me, Dikola's passport if we could get it, and his ticket to England. Once he was here they would pay for a hotel and some clothing for Dikola. I felt like God was answering my prayers.

I couldn't seem to take it all in, and for some reason felt that I could neither trust nor believe it. The next morning I had the paper in my hands. It was really true, Dikola and I had made the front page news. I laughed, I cried. I was a bit surprised by all of the sex bits in it because I knew that the children would be reading it, but we talked about it and I think they handled it rather well, outwardly anyway.

This all seemed an awful lot to take in at seven o'clock in the morning and I can assure you I was not at all prepared for what the rest of the day would bring. My children were wonderful, and stood by me the entire day whilst I hardly had the time to drink a spot of tea. The media interest was overwhelming. The telephone was ringing incessantly from all of the television and radio stations, as well as the newspapers and magazines. We had reporters at the door and news cameras from all over the country.

The Sun was flooded with calls from people wanting to get a piece of the story. I had become a pawn in the media game and didn't know which way to look or what to do. I couldn't seem to think much beyond how all of this was affecting the children and what would happen when Dikola saw it all. So much of it was distanced from the truth and blown out of proportion, I was afraid that he might think I had lied to him.

Stevie and Tommie continued to answer the phone and open the door, talking openly with people about everything. They made tea and drinks and said they really liked all of the excitement and the company. They made me laugh. I realised I had the best kids in the world.

That day I was supposed to work out which morning television show I was going to go on and ended up letting Laura deal with all of it, as I was so lost. We had offers from GMTV, The Big Breakfast, This Morning with Richard and Judy, Good Morning with Anne and Nick, UK Living, Sky TV, Central TV, Thames Sky Holiday Channel, Radio Two, Swahili Radio, IOW Radio, Radio Solent, Radio Four, two German television stations, French and Japanese stations as well as offers from New York for the both of us to go on TV, which had to be turned down because of Dikola's transportation difficulties. I covered as many of these things as possible before I had to leave for my third trip to Kenya and had the rest to deal with upon my return.

Everything was a whirl of activity. In stark contrast to the behaviour of the Big Breakfast, *The Sun* was really wonderful to me, realising the kind of strain I was under. They put me up in a hotel for a few days before I was due to leave for Kenya to give me some much needed rest and keep me away from the prying eyes of the media.

At any rate, all of the attention took my mind largely off how sick I was and gave me something to do and live for again. Something to deal with besides missing and loving a man who was thousands of miles away. It made me fight and gave me the strength to get on to help Dikola, making me a stronger person.

Laura was very good to me, even taking me out one night with her friends so I would not feel neglected. When the time came she took me to the airport.

She wished me well on my journey and gave me a number I could call day or night if I got into any trouble at all. I was also to contact them as soon as I was able to get hold of Dikola's passport as they would be paying for his ticket from their end.

The hospital was not happy about my leaving for Kenya again, but were glad that I was going to go and get Dikola and wished me well.

On the flight to Kenya I had three whole seats to myself and considered myself to be very lucky to have this opportunity to sleep for most of the flight to Mombasa. I was sure God was watching me. It was planned that Dikola would meet me at the airport at midday on the thirteenth of September. It was exactly four months to the day I had left Kenya the last time. It seemed a life time.

I arrived at the appointed meeting point an hour late and saw Dikola and his friend Joseph waiting for me. I walked up to Dikola and we threw our arms around each other, crying. Dikola was shaking. He looked terrible, half starved to death. He had lost weight and was drawn and tired. His hair was not in its normal well kept Masai style and was hidden away in shame. His friend Joseph greeted me with a warm welcome, saying he was glad to have me back as Dikola had been missing me so much he was refusing food.

We made our way back to Mtwapa by taxi. Dikola had booked us into a self contained room with a shower and toilet at the cost of about six pounds a night. It was very clean by the standards of Africa and run by Indians. It was built in with many of the posh vacation bungalows of the white people. I couldn't understand how the owners of these homes could justify their luxurious lives when they were so near to so much suffering.

Dikola suddenly became very ill and I was terrified he might die. I took him to a private hospital in Mombasa which was, again, run by Indians. I knew any treatment he received in a private hospital would be far superior to any we could get in a state run hospital. It was a lovely place, nicer even than any hotel. I stayed with Dikola and was allowed to sleep on a sofa in his room. We even had a private bath with hot water.

The doctor came to speak to me not long after we had arrived, saying he was very worried about Dikola. He felt he was dangerously underweight and undernourished. His body was covered with large scabs and spots. The doctor did not hold out much hope. I couldn't speak and was deeply shocked.

The lady who minds the public toilets was very nice. Sometimes she would call me over to talk to her after I had come out of our flat at six in the morning to use the loo. She thought it odd that we had no toilets in the entire block of flats and was very curious about me.

I told her about when I got to sleep in my own armchair in the front room. This was very good, as before I had to sleep in a studio bed with Jean and my Irish stepfather, making so many odd noises. The chair was all mine, even if it was not very comfortable.

I told her the reason I always seemed so tired was because the household responsibilities were all mine. Washing the clothing at the laundry on the corner, the ironing, care of my younger brother.

She seemed impressed I was only ten.

I knew that this must be some kind of a test from God. I had already spent most of Dikola's passport money on the hospital and had no idea how I would manage to pay for all the rest or if he would even survive long enough for it to become important.

I fell to my knees and prayed to Jesus to help Dikola. After a while I got back up and sat at the edge of Dikola's bed, holding his hand. He drifted in and out of sleep and his temperature was dangerously high.

A lovely black nurse came into the room and saw the moisture of the tears on my cheeks. She smiled at me.

'You have kind eyes,' she said, 'I know when I look at you that you love Jesus. I can feel in you that I am right.' I agreed this was so and she offered to pray with me for a while. She had a great booming voice when she prayed and she loudly demanded that the demons be gone from Dikola's tired body. She begged God to give Dikola the gift of good health and for Dikola to get his passport. She asked that we both make it back to England to get the medical treatment we needed.

I realised only after she had left that I had never said a thing to her about the passport.

I lay awake all night watching Dikola sleep. I didn't move at all and I kept checking on him to make sure that he was still breathing. I drifted off to sleep on the sofa in the early hours of the morning. I awoke to the sound of Dikola calling my name.

'Cheryl, he said, 'Cheryl, I saw Jesus and the twelve disciples. They came to me and talked with me. They walked with me and told me to go in peace and that you would be waiting for me.' I agreed with him that it was truly a wonderful miracle.

That afternoon the doctor reported Dikola's blood test had come up clear and he couldn't understand how his health had changed so quickly for the better. He told me full recovery could be achieved by a few more days of rest and some food. The black nurse came back and the three of us prayed together.

Chapter Eighteen

Later that same day Dikola told me a similar thing had happened to him when he was about sixteen years old. He had been walking with his friends at night across Samburu and had seen an angel in the sky. She was wearing a white dress and had a shining luminescence all around her. He pointed it out to his friends, but they had only laughed and said they certainly had not seen a member of the heavenly host. They all called him crazy.

'Dikola,' I asked, 'did she have wings?'

'Don't be so silly,' he told me, 'angels don't have wings. She just floated there in the black of the night.'

I told him he was very privileged to have seen such a sight, and I wished I could have been there with him. It now made far more sense, our playing angels in Samburu.

Dikola recovered swiftly after this, his skin clearing quickly once he was properly nourished. He was able to wash every day, which he did incessantly. He would spend hours in the shower every day, scrubbing his skin with a loofah. He hated dirt and filth, having lived with it for so long. He loved his clothes and surroundings to be clean, it was such a luxury to him. The time we spent, first in the hospital and then in the hotel, was the most luxury he had ever seen.

I remember him saying that he was upper class, though to me it was still very primitive. It was all so new to him. The first time he went for a hot bath at the hospital he thought the tub was something that was meant for animals.

After we returned to the guest house I had Dikola take me to the place where Emily, my friend from the first trip, was living with her boyfriend Douglas.

When we arrived she was miserable. She was obviously malnourished and wasn't getting enough sleep. She admitted that her periods had become quite bad since her return to Kenya three months previously. She had come over in rose coloured glasses and was now having trouble reconciling the reality with the dreams. She needed to get home to do some down to earth thinking, but had found herself unable to book a flight. She begged for my help.

We went to Mombasa to use the phone to call Nairobi, stopping on the way to buy a phone card. Emily was very bad tempered and highly strung, repeatedly insisting she had already tried calling everywhere and had visited all of the airline offices and had not been able to get a flight home. She was becoming increasingly shrill and verbally abusing Douglas in her frustration.

I begged her to stay calm whilst we tried my way. I called over to Kenya Air in Nairobi, pretending to be the Mombasa branch office. I claimed I had a sick woman at the desk with a medical certificate who desperately needed to get a flight home and medical treatment. They instantly got Emily on a flight leaving the next morning at two o'clock.

We saw her off at the airport, leaving in time for her tearful farewell to Douglas.

We had already started the long and complicated process of getting the passport for Dikola. Luckily the laws had changed since the last time I inquired about getting the passport and we were no longer required to go all the way to Nairobi to apply and were able to take care of it in Mombasa.

It was a twenty mile bus trip to and from the office, a trip which we made once, sometimes even twice a day. I was afraid I was going to have to ask for some extra cash from Mike because our money was already getting low from Dikola's illness and, though the passport only cost fifteen pounds officially, it could end up costing hundreds of pounds. I knew Toni had spent six hundred pounds on a passport she never even got, not knowing how to play the system. It is an organisation which demands the utmost respect from citizens and tourists alike and has to be treated very cautiously. We knew we would have to be very patient.

After much persuading we were finally allowed to see the High Commissioner of Mombasa to plead our case before him. I was told he was a very intimidating man. I was a bundle of nerves as I went to see him, knowing he was our one real hope of getting the documentation we so desperately needed. I took a photograph of my children to try to soften his heart a bit. I knew I would only have a very limited amount of time with this man. Dikola kept on insisting there was no way I was going to be able to get this man's signature, as it always took at least six months to get it on anything. I told him to trust in God.

I put the photograph on the desk in front of the official and he snapped at me, asking my business. I told him I wanted Dikola to come home with me on the thirty first of October. I said I was missing my children and I wanted Dikola to come home with me to show them what a good life they have. I claimed he was a friend I had met when there on holiday previously and had promised my children I would bring him home. I begged him not to make me a liar. I told him I was a regular tourist in this part of the world and had found Dikola to be a wonderful protector, as I always wanted to see the wilder parts of Africa, the real Africa.

With that he stamped my form and threw it at me. Before I left him I insisted once again that I really needed to get home by that final day of October. He softened a little and gave me the name of the person I should contact next, saying I should use his name when I did. With that I hastily thanked him, leaving his office triumphant.

During this time all of the warriors began to call me by my Masai name 'Nicmarie.' They said I had managed to do what no one else had; getting the world to recognise who the Samburu Masai are. They thought of Dikola and I as heroes and besides, it gave them another story and they love nothing better.

We have just moved into our new house; me, Richelle, Mum and my stepfather. It is nicer than our last home, and much bigger. It is also in horrible condition and my stepfather says it needs a lot of work. He thinks it would be best if we start in the bathroom.

Mum went out yesterday to buy some wallpaper, but my stepfather needs help putting it up and Mum doesn't want to do it. My stepfather asks me to help.

We aren't very good at papering, and my stepfather is getting increasingly angry and frustrated. I try not to make him angry. I know how grown-ups can get when they are in a mood like this.

My stepfather sits down on the toilet, tiring of the task. He grabs me by my shoulders and slams my stomach between his open legs. I try to scream, but am breathless.

During this trip we made two significant friends, Heather and Neil.

Dikola was having his hair done in the Masai style. It would take three men five days to finish it, working from around eight-thirty in the morning until almost six.

On some of these days I would come down with them and tell stories or read to them. They would use me as a runner to go and get them soft drinks and food. People would pass making comments about the white woman and the warriors. I didn't mind as it made room for conversation.

On one of these days I was starting to feel a little claustrophobic and bored of my position of gopher. I let Dikola know I was going to go off to read a book I had on Africa and would be sitting outside the local bar. The word went out that I would be there and was to be checked on and protected as a friend of the Masai. I had nothing to fear.

I found a spot on a rocky wall outside the bar and put my feet up. I opened my bottle of warmed Tuska and settled into my book. I had begun to desperately miss English companionship. I was growing tired of constantly having to explain what I was saying. The book was my refuge from a world that to me was still hostile.

I had been reading for around three hours when I heard the sweet voices of singing children. They were marching up the street and towards me, passing with the greeting 'Jambo Mazungu', Hi white person. I smiled and returned their greetings.

I looked over to my right and saw two white women come out of the bar, one blonde and one brunette. I was anxious for their safety in this part of Mombasa and also hopeful that they might be British, and approached them.

I asked them if they were British and they confirmed they were. They appeared to be as concerned for my safety as I was for theirs and asked if I was alone, explaining, as I knew, that it was not safe in this area.

They invited me to come to the bar to join them in a drink. They both had their husbands with them as well as a black bodyguard hired from the hotel they were staying in. I drew up a seat to join them in a beer or two.

The blonde one, Heather, was with Neil and they turned out to be a very pleasant couple. The other couple turned their nose up at me, and I returned the compliment.

They were surprised by how many people were greeting me and I would explain who each one was in turn. 'Oh, he is a policeman. He owns the Masai Cafe. That one is a little crazy because he was too clever and could not find a job to match his mind.' Everybody found this to be very amusing and thought it would all make great stories for the office.

After a while a tall Masai warrior turned up at the table looking down on me as if I was a naughty toddler. He was in full warrior gear with his spear and everything. Heather laughed nervously, unsure of this change in situation.

'Dikola sent me,' said the tall warrior, Simon, 'all warriors have been looking for you. It was reported that you had gone missing from the outside of this bar. Dikola said you must come, he wants you now.' Heather became even more nervous.

I told Simon to send Dikola to me and tell him I would be waiting with some white people whom I had found to speak with and should be quite safe. He hesitated for a moment, gave me a long look and left.

When he left, Heather and Neil demanded to know what it was all about. I explained to them that I was the woman who had been in the press so much and they knew instantly who I was. An even better story for the office.

Neil said he would very much like to meet Dikola and I reported he would be coming over around six-thirty if they would like to meet him that evening. They explained that they did not want to be here after dark but would like it if they could catch up with us at an alternative time.

I had the feeling that they did not think Dikola was a real person because they had had a few drinks and thought my story was too far fetched to be true. I promised to bring Dikola to their hotel the next morning so they could meet the man themselves.

I explained that we usually kept away from the beaches and hotels because so many of the tourists recognised us and we felt better keeping a low profile. We heard stories about people coming all the way to Kenya just to try and meet us.

The next day we did make an exception to go to their hotel. Dikola was in full warrior dress. As we walked towards Heather and Neil, we surprised Heather so badly that she missed the food on her fork and dropped it back onto her plate, mouth open in amazement. They hadn't really thought I would come.

After an hour or so the strain lifted a little. They took some photos and shot a little video. Dikola wouldn't smile until later when we were all feeling a bit more comfortable and were drinking beers down on the beach and talking. I was glad Dikola was making friends with British people.

We made arrangements for them to come with us to Mtwapa. They preferred the atmosphere and the element of danger. When it was time to leave Dikola and I agreed to escort them back.

We boarded yet another bone shaker of a bus and Neil became apprehensive whilst Heather just giggled nervously. I wondered that I hadn't been like her when I first came.

We spent a lot of time together on their balcony and sometimes having hotel dinners together. We had some good laughs together and thought it was very funny when Dikola tried using the video camera. He got some very good shots of our feet, ears and hands.

The last evening we spent with them I remember taking some footage of Dikola on the balcony. When I looked at him through the view finder I wanted to cry. He looked so helpless and childlike. I wanted to cry, but was with company, so I laughed instead.

Our last toast of that evening Heather made to seeing Dikola and I in England five years from now, knowing full well how difficult it is to get a passport. How surprised they would be.

Despite all the good friends and good atmosphere around us at night, I was starting to get very edgy and was drinking far too much in the evenings. More and more people were feeling at liberty to come up to me and ask for a few shillings at a time. As time wore on I was finding it harder and harder to keep up with the demand as my funds were very limited. It was an enormous burden already, without having to watch my funds drain away again, for the second time in this dangerous country. The beer was only thirty five pence a bottle and it seemed well worth it to help dull the pain and anxiety a bit.

The passport business was very long and drawn out and based on so many rootless promises. We had filled out all of the forms required and passed the five different interviews administered by five different officers. Things seemed to be going smoothly, and we were only being made to pay the standard fee, which was a great relief, but still we had no passport.

It was a bit of a Catch 22 situation in that you could not have a passport without a plane ticket and were not allowed to get a plane ticket without a passport. Finally I was able to get through to *The Sun* and have them buy a ticket, a process which took several trips to the town to use the telephone before they finally understood the system as well as I did.

They paid for a month's return ticket through Kenya Air, and through this I was able to get a letter certifying that it existed in Dikola's name. We had fulfilled all of the requirements.

Time and money were running short. I had gone over with fourteen hundred pounds and only had seven thousand shillings left as the exchange rate had halved against my favour in the time I had been in the country. To make it until it was time to leave I would have to get more money from England. Mike came to my rescue again.

Just as we thought we were going to get clearance on the passport the CID came to investigate Dikola. One meeting after the other was required of us and the strain was starting to show. I started to lose hope, thinking all of our efforts were slipping through our fingers.

I was becoming violent towards Dikola again, throwing beer bottles and screaming. He was very calm and gentle and would say in deep, measured tones 'If you were a man I would hit you. I would never lay a finger on you.' All of my other boyfriends, and even gentle Mike, had managed to hit me on occasion, and I was stunned and placated by Dikola's complete lack of violent tendencies against me. I kept on pushing harder and harder, seeing how far I could go before he would either leave or hit back. Once I said to him the nastiest thing I could think of, and, upon receiving no reaction, hit him in his side with his rungu.

I was shocked by my behaviour and dropped the rungu, guilty. He knelt on the floor, doubled over in pain. Finally he looked up, saying 'I cannot hit you back. Maybe one day you will understand it. If it makes you happy to beat me like a dog, go ahead. I love you.'

His words twisted inside me like a knife and I was sure that this marked the end of our relationship together. I fled to the nearest bar to get drunk. All the time that I was busy getting drunk, Dikola was watching me, though I did not know it. He wanted to make sure no harm would come to me. Finally he approached and said he forgave me, but to please refrain from such behaviour in the future.

The next night I decided to get Dikola drunk. It wasn't hard, he was so light and was not used to large quantities of alcohol. I had hoped that having him drunk would loosen his tongue, to test if he loved me and why. I thought that the drink would reveal any secrets that he might have. I seemed to never be able to stop testing him.

My little trick on him backfired and he became very emotional, revealing an extremely loving person under his staunch exterior. He spoke of his siblings and his parents and all of the love and respect he had for all of them. He talked about the strain of having them all depend on him, still so young. The burdens he had to carry were all so heavy. I felt horribly guilty for ever having doubting his sincerity. He became terribly ill because of the large quantities of the stuff he had consumed. I nursed him through the night. I would never consider doing such a horrible thing to him again.

We only had three days left on Dikola's ticket. The CID man had slowed things down for us horribly and I had to go to the passport office once again to see if anything could possibly be done. The head of the department told me that if I could get the tickets for Dikola, he would get the passport. I scheduled our flight for the thirty-first at seven-thirty in the evening. The last possible time out, a Monday.

That weekend was the longest ever and Dikola and I spent most of it in bed. I knew that with or with out Dikola I would have to fly out on Monday. All of my money was gone except what would get us through the weekend in food and drink and airport tax.

Monday came, scorching hot and neither Dikola nor I spoke. We awoke early for what we hoped would be our final trip to the passport office. This was our last chance. I had not even packed anything, fearing it would be bad luck. We were told to go back once more at two-thirty to pick up the passport.

Dikola was convinced by now that there was no way we were going to get it. We had some time to kill so we went back into Mtwapa to get a little to eat. Finally we went back to the office, getting there fifteen minutes past the appointed time to give them a little extra time. They were true to their word and we had a passport.

Now we were in a rush to get back to the hotel, get our things, say our goodbyes and pick up the ticket at the airline office in time to catch the plane. Most people didn't even know our plans as we had been very secretive, superstitiously. They were all shocked.

Chapter Nineteen

Some of the warriors came with us to say goodbye, and before we knew it we were on the plane on our way to Nairobi. Dikola was very good about flying, despite our having separate seats. He marvelled at our reaching Nairobi in an hour, as he was used to it taking eight hours by coach. After we got off the plane he kept on talking about how clever planes were and simply couldn't get over it.

We had a very easy trip from there to home, with me telling Dikola what he could expect in England. He couldn't fully understand what I was talking about, but I prepared him as best as I could. He thought the landing was fascinating, coming down through the light cloud cover and seeing all of the little English houses dotted around the country.

We got through passport control just fine and had to catch the tube to Rotherhith. All of this high tech travel in one day was quite a lot for Dikola to swallow and I knew that he was a bit overwhelmed. The strain started to show particularly when a man on the tube started to chat Dikola up thinking that he was a girl. Another black man came to push the Indian man off, and Dikola and I were just able to escape before things became too heated.

My friend and I are coming back from the football match at Crystal Palace. It wasn't much fun, but the company was good. There are some older boys on the train with us, but the carriage is empty besides. They are starting to tease us, taunt us. My friend isn't frightened, but then, it is me they are focusing most of the attention on. They come and sit close to us. My friend is very calm. I am terrified.

One of the boys unscrews a bulb from the ceiling and is threatening to burn me if I don't cooperate with him. I am paralysed with fear. My friend does nothing to help me. She keeps laughing at the 'joke,' yet her voice is shriller. The train pulls into the station and my friend is able to get off. I am trapped under three of the men before I can follow my friend onto the platform. They are ripping at my clothes and my hair. I am too frightened to scream.

Suddenly, one of the boys starts to pull the others off me, saying I looked terrified and they mustn't force me. I escape just as the train is pulling away. Some nasty girls from school are on the platform when I get off. They think that I liked it.

At Rotherhith Laura came to pick us up in her car and take us to the Docklands Hotel. It was situated on the River Thames and certainly Dikola had never seen such luxury. It was a lot for him to handle. Good food and drink were available for us just by picking up the phone. Dikola had never had so much for so little. A long photo shoot for *The Sun* hardly seemed adequate compensation. They took us first class all the way.

We went to the Isle of Wight for a day and a half for another photo session with *The Sun*, and Dikola's initial impressions were good. Chloie and Dikola got on right away and played like children together. Mike, Tommie and Stevie all did their bit also.

Afterwards we went back to London to the hotel for more questions and stories, as well as photos of us in London and fashion shoots.

For one of the photos the photographer wanted Dikola to pose in full Masai gear in the November weather, going up and down an escalator. I refused, as it would look so foolish and it was cold out. We spent two weeks in the hotel whilst they prepared the story.

Our friends Heather and Neil began to hear all of the stories in the news and made a beeline to contact us. We still see them to this day and are great friends.

The television stations began to contact us, and once again we were travelling, talking to all of the television stations and staying in posh hotels. We rented a single attic room in Newport as our base because all of the money from the television stations was going to pay the debt I had accumulated as well as to buy some clothing for Dikola as he had so little.

Most of the TV stations asked us if we would marry, a question which I refused to answer. Dikola was only on a six months visitor's visa and I knew that we could not get the visa we needed from Nairobi from this end and were terrified to return after all of the hassle of going last time.

By the time Christmas came around I knew I would have to get a flat so my children could stay with me, should they wish to. I was able to get a flat in Cowes, but had to take social security money to do so, something it seemed I had no choice but to do. It was a better situation because it meant that the children could visit and I would no longer have to go around Mike's to do the cooking and washing. I liked the idea of being completely independent from him and getting my own life. It was now time to try to pick up some of the pieces of the relationship with my children. I feared I had already torn down too much of their trust to be to them what I had been previously. I knew they were being tormented at school because of what I had done and could only hope they wouldn't be too damaged.

Finally it was time to set a date for the wedding. On a year from the day that we met we set our first date, a red herring to elude the press, of the thirteenth of January. We then changed it to Valentine's Day, after cancelling the first date. Apparently our dupe failed as the entire world seemed to be there to witness the small gathering on the Isle of Wight.

For the ceremony we once again handed ourselves over to *The Sun* for media protection. They were able to put us up in a lovely hotel. We did another long photo session, this time with both Stevie and Chloie present.

A woman I barely knew was kind enough to lend us her 1927 Bentley for the occasion. We felt so rich that day.

The big day was somewhat lost because of all of the media attention, but still we were well cared for. Vicky was taking care of us this time as Laura was at home taking care of her new baby daughter. She did well keeping us fed and watered and generally comfortable.

At this time both of us were in good health, Dikola having had the same virus as I had, but in its more manageable form.

The night before a crew from GMTV came to set up for the next morning. The woman in charge was very good to us, the first television person to really treat Dikola like a human being and he appreciated this very much and was well at ease with her, despite being too embarrassed to do some of his famous Masai jumping. We did some filming that night, staying up until after one in the morning, despite knowing we would have to be up again at six thirty for a live link up.

As the morning approached we barely slept, we were so nervous. That day we were expecting film crews from Germany, as well as Meridian TV, ITN and BBC South. I had told the others we simply couldn't cope with them and would speak no further. We spent most of the night talking and tossing and turning. We were truly famous for a day and it was frightening.

The next morning after we did our bit for GMTV they gave us a champagne breakfast. Then it was the turn of the German crew and they seemed to follow us around almost everywhere. It made us both edgy having a camera on us all during our wedding day. I suppose I should have been better about wedding jitters, having done it twice before, but somehow I wasn't. This was different. I was looking forward to becoming Mrs. Lekimenju, a member of the Lmasula Clan, the largest of the Samburu. It was like becoming part of the most primitive people that time had preserved; joining an exclusive club. Dikola made me special. I had found my identity.

We pulled up as scheduled in front of the council chambers on Valentine's Day in the deep green Bentley. We were freezing in our traditional Masai dress. Chloie was dressed in a similar manner, as I had made her an outfit for the occasion. We were all very colourful in our bright red clothing. She was holding a bunch of roses and looked an absolute peach. I was so very proud to have her by my side.

A cheering crowd greeted us at the meeting point. A group of girls kept on calling to Dikola to show them his bum, making him smile. My left breast was threatening to fall out of my kanga as I was bravely braless.

Cameras and photographers were all around us, reporters had come from all over the world just for this one day. I had no idea who to talk to first. We were so cold in our clothing and just wanted to get inside. We had dressed this way for what it symbolised and to let Dikola's people know we had not forgotten them. We wanted to feel that, though they may be far away in body, they were close in spirit. Our clothes represented him and his way of life. It didn't matter to us that the weather was freezing.

After the few niceties we made it into the council chambers to cement the bonds that tied us. My first wedding was a full church wedding, all in white. My second was in a registry office, me in an emerald green dress. This one was in council chambers with each of us wearing only a three pound Kanga and beads. It meant far more to me than either of the others had. It was magical and wonderful. I felt like a nervous little girl. It was really me getting married this time, not some woman whom others expected me to be.

Chapter Twenty

Before the ceremony Dikola and I turned to greet our guests. I saw Toni there, her eyes bright with mockery. She had brought with her Luria, Dikola's cousin and another Samburu man named James who was a priest on sponsorship to England.

I was glad to have at least two of Dikola's people with us on this day, but pitied that they would not have been there if it had not been for Toni, as we were still, as ever, having some difficulties in our relationship. I didn't bother to ponder why she was there. I was simply so happy to be marrying the man I loved.

We exchanged our vows, kissed and turned to smile for the cameras. We departed quickly for the reception on a cloud of cheery congratulations.

Outside the council chambers we were greeted with more clicks of cameras and cheers from well wishers. We would have stayed longer to chat, but though our hearts were warm, it was still quite cold outside. We had a wonderful party for the reception with a band and all of the trimmings.

Our wedding cake was a brown and white heart with the word 'asham' written across it. There are those who have thought that it was English, 'a sham,' but really it means 'to love' in Maa.

To celebrate the day we bought a pair of peach faced love birds and had each others names tattooed on our right breasts. We had our ears pierced with the stones of love.

This afternoon, during the warm season, my mother and I are in the back yard, leaning against the window sill. She is wearing a light blue shirt, with a small pocket on the left breast, which she begins to speak to quietly.

'Come on, come out, there's a good girl,' she whispers gently into her blue pocket. I look on, slightly dazed, surely little good can come of being chummy with the left breast pocket of your blue shirt?

As I stare at Mum, who was eagerly eying her shirt front, a little ladybird comes scuttling out of her pocket. I am struck by the feeling that she is really talking to it and more, that it understood. It is like watching Father Christmas land.

I watch as the ladybird scampers over her shirt. Mum tells me that the red and black insect had landed on her injured, and she had put it into her pocket to recover a few days ago. With a reassuring word, she scoops the small beast onto the tip of her finger and urges it to fly away. It stays. Mum blows on her finger gently and the wee creature opens its wings and flies, stopping briefly on Mum's shirt for a final thank you.

We went to Scotland for our honeymoon and Dikola touched snow for the first time. His eyes were full of wonderment. We saw the reindeer and The Electric Water Theatre, all full of lights and colour. Dikola was sure the ice skaters were on wheels until he touched the blade himself. All of these wonderful and unforgettable memories. It opened up a new world for me also and I felt like I was seeing it all for the first time.

There were so many well wishers from all over the country, we thank everybody for their support.

I believe that me deep connection with Dikola and my erratic and even destructive behaviour of the past can be explained by my traumatic childhood.

Perhaps my feelings about my youth are best summed up a poem I sent to my Mum on a recent birthday.

To find a birthday card Mum,
That tells you how I feel,
I'd have to search the whole world through

And not find a verse that fit.
Cards with flowers, puppy dogs and kittens
Words inside that I have never felt.
So I sit and try to write the words
Read them back and then again.
The truth is, Mum; or is it Jean?
There is no real love that I have seen
As a child, not a cuddle or a kiss
My teens you stole and used
Inside I feel the pain.
You wrenched me, tore me broke me down
I thought I'd go insane.
As a woman you fear me and what I have to say.
I see it in your eyes; the truth you hide away.
You store it in your whiskey
And mask your lies with fumes
For your mind and your survival,
There is no other way.
For you I turn to God and pray.
Forgive our sins from day to day.
God Forgive and Bless You.

Living with child abuse is like being bound to a rotting corpse. The stench clings to you like octopus suckers. You can constantly taste it, smell it, see it. It rots your mind like alcohol rots your liver. It permeates your thoughts. As you age you continue to read sex into every situation. You may give off or read the wrong signals, thereby rendering everybody a sexual beast in your mind. The adult constantly tries to put sex in its proper spot. Terribly frightened of the physical aspects of love while desperately requiring the warmth and compassion. Love and sex. Sex and love. It seems too often that fitting the two together is like breast feeding in sexy lingerie; it can be done but one does not typically feel the need to do so.

Dikola is my harbour from my memories. My safety. There are times when past phantoms become too strong and I cry again for my shattered childhood. Dikola cries with me, never judging. He washes my hands, massaging them with scented oils, kissing my palms until I smile. He soothes my tear-warmed cheeks with cool kisses, reminding me of my innocence. This is part of the love I found in Kenya.

Our friend Emily returned to Kenya one last time to try and make one last go of things with Douglas. Unfortunately, it turned out to be a terrible mistake for her. I was in England at the time and only heard the story second hand.

Douglas had been a wreck when Emily left the first time; I knew this first hand as I had been there for a while after she left. He had disappeared for over a week after she left.

The last time she came over attempting to make some kind of a go of the relationship, Douglas had stolen two thousand pounds out of her bag, thereby forcing her to go home early.

I would like to think that he was not responsible, particularly since he was the only one of the Masai to ever return borrowed money to me, but all of the evidence is there. He was the only one with the key to where Emily was lodging and people had seen him leaving the building with all of her things. He has not been seen since.

Emily has since left for a job in Dallas, Texas and we keep in touch and wish each other well. She still has very deep feelings for Douglas and asks for any news of him each time we speak.

Today we are living on the knife's edge not knowing if we will be allowed to be together in this, the country of my children's birth. If it were not for them I would leave England. I would find my life in Kenya, as this country and all of its trappings has ceased to have any hold on me.

Dikola and I currently live together in a rented flat in Cowes. Our landlord and his wife are good to us and have made us welcome in a flat they are currently not using, due to the high rate of unemployment on the island.

We live a very normal, happy life, cycling and walking to save money. We look after the children as best we can, though cannot currently offer them any kind of accommodation. They have told me that they wish to spend more time with me and Dikola, and I am trying to do this one small thing for them to make up for the hurt that I have caused them. I pray I find the right path for them.

Our problems now seem to us mountain high. I don't know if Dikola will be allowed to stay longer than his papers indicate and we are living waiting for the answer day to day. There are an awful lot of people out there who have tried to help us in this way. If you are one of them, I thank you. I fear that our solicitor is not holding out much hope.

I will close our story here. It is not the end, simply part of a long waiting period with the Home Office. It is something Dikola and I have become accustomed to. We sit and pray for this marriage that God made, may it not be broken. It is not the end. Only another beginning. I know that someday we will be free.

Editor's Note:

Just prior to the printing of this book, Cheryl and Dikola were given the news that Dikola is to be 'removed' back to Kenya.

Because the couple are leaving for Africa in three days, it is my privilege to write this final entry.

Dikola has been asked to leave the country because he and Cheryl had been unable to obtain the proper visa from the Kenyan authorities prior to returning from their last trip to Kenya in October of last year.

Cheryl has been on sickness and housing benefits to support the couple since her separation from her second husband, Mike Mason. One of the requirements from the Home Office is that Cheryl and Dikola be able to support themselves without the benefit of the state before Dikola be allowed to stay. Had they been able to fulfil this requirement, as well as obtained the visa, Dikola would have been able to remain in the country.

It is worth noting that Dikola has been offered a position as an assistant to a photographer and Cheryl is now capable of housing herself, as the house she shared with her children and previous husband has been sold and she will retain half of the proceeds. She is capable of working part time despite her history of ill health.

The earliest Dikola will be allowed into the country is six months from the time he leaves.

To the best of the knowledge of myself and my colleagues who have aided me in the production of this book, Cheryl intends to stay with Dikola in Kenya until the middle of October, at which time she will return to continue her struggle.